# STANDING ON THE SHOULDERS

*A Legacy Story of a Father, a Son, and Life's Greatest Gifts*

## Tim Brand

*Foreword by*
*Tommy Spaulding*

At the author's request, all royalties due to the author will benefit Many Hands' work with mothers and children in need, who need someone's shoulders to stand on for a season.

Library of Congress Control Number: 2023924107

ISBN: 979-8-9891365-0-6 (Hard Cover);
979-8-9891365-1-3 (Paperback)

Printed in the United States of America

*To my kids, nephews, nieces, and the generations to come.*
*May you know Grandpa's story, as you dream a little bigger*
*and love a little deeper because of his life well lived.*

# Foreword

There are words in the English vocabulary that are drastically overused by westerners. One word that comes to mind: Love. I lived in Japan for two years teaching English when I was in my twenties. The thing I appreciated most about the Japanese culture and language is that the word *love* is sacred. Sacred. The word is never used unless a Japanese person REALLY means it. I love you. Or Aishiteru, as the Japanese say it. Sacred.

Westerners say and use the word *love* probably more than any word in the dictionary. I love Italian food. I love vacationing in Florida. I love the New York Yankees. I love ice cream. Overused.

When I first met Tim Brand, back in December 2017, I did not know then that he would not only change the way I used the word *love,* but more importantly, changed the way I lived the word *love*.

Six years ago, I was coaching and mentoring a high school student, who also happened to be named Tommy. I wanted to give

Tommy a "life changing" experience that would influence his heart forever. An experience that would make him realize what a blessed life he had and understand the power of serving others. My dear friends Jon and Stacie Sefton introduced me to an organization called Many Hands for Haiti based out of Pella, Iowa. This organization worked with volunteers who served the poor in Haiti. Two months later, Tommy and I planned a service trip to Haiti. Thanks to the help of my new friend, Tim Brand, we planned a "life changing" trip that would help this young high school kid become a heart-led leader.

The night before the early morning trip to Haiti, Tommy canceled. I had a choice to make. Should I cancel my trip as well or honor the hard work Tim and his team had planned and attend the trip solo? I got on the plane the next morning and my life has never been the same.

Haiti is only 682.23 miles by plane from Miami, Florida. A mere two-hour flight separates one of the richest countries in the world from one of the poorest. What I learned from my very first Haitian friend, Louisa, a janitor at the Many Hands for Haiti campus is this: Haitians may be poor financially, but they are wealthy with love. And love is far more valuable.

Tim Brand taught me more about love in that five-day trip to Haiti, than all my years on this planet. Now, we all get to learn from Tim's beautiful heart as he shares that love in the book you are now holding in your hands. Standing on the Shoulders is about one word: Aishiteru…LOVE! A love between a father and a son. A love between man and his community. And, more importantly, a love between Jesus and His followers.

Of the 36,000 words in Tim's book, there are thirty-two words that will change your life and influence the remaining years you have living on this planet.

"Will those who come behind you need to fix all the things you broke during your life, or will they stand on foundations you built, stronger because of the way you lived?"

Tim Brand has stood tall on the shoulders of his father, Denny Brand, for his entire life and continues to stand on the shoulders of his legacy. Denny was not famous or wealthy and his death did not make the headlines or national news. However, Denny did something most of us fail to do. Denny lived a life of giving, serving, and loving. So much so that the entire community of Pella, Iowa, and all who knew him will never be the same.

After Tim tells you Denny's story, you too will stand a little taller and your life will never be the same.

*Tommy Spaulding*
*September 2023*

# TABLE OF CONTENTS

# INTRODUCTION

There is a question each of us need to wrestle with:

"Will those who come behind you need to fix all the things you broke during your life or will they stand on foundations you built, stronger because of the way you lived?"

I didn't become who I am today on my own. None of us do. Rather, I stood on the shoulders of my dad, who lived in such a way for me to see farther, stand firmer, and love deeper. His life through small actions had legacy power. And because of this, many lives have been changed forever.

Dad was not famous, and his death didn't make the national news. Yet, he lived a joyful, remarkable life, and his impact was deeply felt by those who knew him. What does a good life look like? I point to Dad's life as he was as real as it gets to the people he loved. And people loved him for it.

None of us like to talk about the end of life. Sons and daughters do not want to say goodbye to their mom or dad. Unfortunately, life doesn't give us a choice. How do you show up in hardship and still bring hope? How do you guide those final moments and help loved ones finish well?

I wrote this book to give the world a glimpse into this journey for my family and me, as I believe God's face shined during that time. We were faithful through this difficult season, and God was faithful in return. And as strange as this sounds, we found life in death. I've never experienced life in the full as much as I have walking through death. And we know Dad is experiencing an abundant life beyond the grave. How can this be? It is one of life's paradoxes, a great mystery to be unwrapped.

As you read this book, I want you to think about your dash. All of us have a dash between two numbers. For me, this will be 1979 – 20XX. For my dad, this was 1943 – 2021. How will you use your dash? What gifts have you been given? What gifts will you leave for others?

To begin with the end in mind is a blessing, not a curse. To live a life a son or daughter can build upon is one of the greatest gifts a parent can give a child. To see your own story woven into something greater – there is peace in that process. This is what the book is all about.

# The Gift of Commitment

Waking up on the morning of Friday, October 29, 2021, I'm more nervous than normal. Today is the third annual Many Hands Business Breakfast, but because of COVID-19, we haven't had this event for two years. The Community Choice Credit Union Convention Center in downtown Des Moines is a beautiful setting, comfortably sitting 300 of Des Moines' best and brightest leaders. *Challenge What's Possible* is the theme and oh, does it hit the mark for what was soon coming for me and my family. Little did I know how this theme would become my mantra as I walked my dad home during his final six weeks of life on earth.

My dad, Denny Brand, wakes up that same October morning and doesn't feel well. He wants to come to the Many Hands Business Breakfast with his beautiful bride of 56 years, but the energy isn't there. Over the past five years, Dad has been battling a rare blood cancer called Myelofibrosis. It has robbed his bones of the ability to create red blood cells, so oxygen doesn't course through his body, causing him to be incredibly tired. Stumbling into the shower, Dad notices his right foot is hurting. He glances down and sees a very thin black line between his big toe and second toe. This isn't normal and dang, is it tender. Getting out of the shower and into his clothes, he plops down in his Lazy-boy chair. Tired and spent for the day, he shoots me a text, "Wish I could be there. Praying for you."

I don't receive this text until after the Business Breakfast as I was immersed in the whirl of the morning. As my dad was losing energy, I was gaining it. Events like this make me come alive. Feeling the buzz of the crowd, shaking hands, exchanging smiles, and the big-bear hugs to friends you haven't seen in a while – I love it all. Being on stage has never bothered me. The bigger the crowd, the more I want to be there and this morning, this was exactly where I needed to be.

Getting up on stage, I look over the crowd and spot my mom and my twenty-year-old nephew, Nolan, Dad's replacement for the morning. A moment of disappointment washes over me because I felt this morning would have energized him. It's not to be.

Dad loved people, and he especially loved the people of Haiti, having taken his first trip in 1986. I grew up looking at a picture of him on that first trip. Sitting on the back of a well-worn donkey, this 43-year-old man is ascending a winding, rocky path toward a fortress called the Citadelle. At 6 '1", 200 pounds, black with gray-streaked hair, you can just sense the sweat dripping down his back, and he is wildly out of place. Wearing a straw hat, he is the only white person in the picture, flanked by two young men of darker complexion. Over that past week, he had spent time in a small, rural community in the central plateau of Haiti called

Pignon. He had come with members of his local Iowa church, hearing about this opportunity through colleagues and friends. He left his wife and three children at home, to seek God's will by serving in the poorest country in the Western Hemisphere. Now, here I am 34 years later, on a grand stage, leading a non-profit serving these same people God had placed on Dad's heart so many years ago.

"I don't believe it is randomness as to why you are here," I kick off my opening talk. "I believe God has brought you to the Community Choice Credit Union on October 29, 2021, for a purpose. And the gift of this morning will be revealed over time – some will get their gift quickly and others will have to wait a bit. But I can promise, if you are present this morning, there is something special for you today."

At the time, I don't realize how much I am talking to myself.

"What used to be simple has somehow become complicated," I share. I immediately think of Dad and his struggles of late. Going to a sporting event, parking a car, and walking to sit in the bleachers used to be simple. Now, it is complicated. Seeing someone on the street, shaking their hand, and talking to them used to be simple. Now, it is complicated. Simply leaving the house and not worrying about if you could make it to a restroom used to be simple. Now, it is complicated.

"Before moving forward this morning, we need to address where we really are. We must confront the brutal facts in our life, putting a stake in the ground and saying, 'Yes, this is where we are at today,'" I share with the audience. "Each of us brings wounded voices in our heads telling us on repeat everything wrong. And when we think about what is possible, many default to the wounded voice of everything impossible, rather than thinking what is possible."

The brutal facts for me that morning seem impossible. Dad has been given a diagnosis of cancer five years ago, with a life expectancy of three- to five years. We are playing with borrowed time. Another brutal fact, my dad is not in the crowd this morning because he doesn't have enough energy to leave his house. Heck, he can barely walk to his chair.

"Let's own it this morning. On a piece of paper, write down the broken voice in your head. It is super important to write it down. Whatever is on your heart this morning, I want you to write it down. Now, here is our promise to one another. Leave this wounded voice on the table for the next hour. Don't pick it up and keep your mind open to possibilities. Can you promise me this?"

During the next hour, love in action pours out of our speakers. My friend John O'Leary delivers an amazing keynote, sharing all the adversity he has overcome in his life and how it has shaped his thinking. We share a video of Pastor Jean Ronel's story, of surviving the 2010 Port-au-Prince earthquake and how it shaped him to courageously serve those affected by the 2021 Les Cayes earthquake, despite the grave dangers. At one point, we had 102,000 pounds of food to deliver to people in need but to get there, the trucks needed to travel through gang-infested roads known for violence and kidnapping. When asked if anyone could go, knowing it could potentially take his life, Jean Ronel raised his hand and said, "I'll be the one."

I come back up on stage, full of emotion and awe of the incredible stories we have just witnessed, to deliver the closing remarks. "As we wrap up our time together, I want to come back to some words Jean Ronel shared with us. He said, 'The impossibility is in our mind. We have to overcome that. And this is what Many Hands does.' Take a look at that wounded voice you wrote down on that piece of paper at the beginning of our time together."

My wounded voice: *This can't end well.* How is it even possible to end well, when cancer takes and takes and takes?

"You have two options right now – you can pick it back up again, carry it with you, like a weight on your shoulders. Or, you can heal it, rewriting it based on what's possible. It is your choice at this point. I pray you have the courage to heal this wounded voice and live into your possibilities. You are at a Many Hands event and this is what we do, so I can promise you that you can do it, too. Take time right now to write your healed voice statement."

With intentionality, I write my healed voice statement: *We choose life. Life on Dad's terms and in God's timing. This is not the end.*

"Earlier, you heard Jean Ronel answer the question, 'Can someone go?' with the response, 'I'll be the one.' Where do you need to be 'the one' right now?"

I add to my healed voice statement: *I'll be the one to help Dad finish well.*

The entire audience ends the meeting raising their hands and saying, "I'll be the one." What a beautiful morning!

Unfortunately, as the day goes on for my dad, his foot gets significantly worse. The blackness starts to spread and the pain grows. Mom calls and asks if I can bring over a medical scooter for the weekend since Dad isn't able to put weight on the foot.

"Sure, I'll be the one to bring over the scooter for Dad." That was a pretty easy response given the declarations spoken earlier.

On Sunday of that same week, I preach at church and am exhausted from a very long couple of days. However, I know the right thing to do is to take our family to Mom and Dad's place that evening to visit. Sitting and talking to Dad with his foot up on a pillow, I have an overwhelming sense that this might be the last time we are all together like this. After dinner, I look more closely at Dad's foot.

"Yikes, that looks pretty bad. Why is it so red and swollen?" I ask.

"I don't know. It probably is just a broken blood vessel or something and now blood is in there. I don't want to go to the hospital, as they just poke me and send me home," Dad grumbles.

"I know. But, you don't want that to get much worse. Otherwise, we have bigger issues and we should nip this in the bud as soon as possible. It is your call, but I'd go see someone tomorrow," I push a bit.

"We will see what happens tonight. This sucker hurts, I know that," he claims.

We say our goodbyes and I love you's as is accustomed in our family when departing. "You know my mom could never say I love you," Dad tells me. "That is why I always want to say it to you."

"I know, Dad. I love you, too. Keep me updated and we will keep praying for you," I say as I walk out the door.

Getting into the car, I look at my wife, Catie, and say, "This is not good. I just have a feeling about this one. I know we've been through some scares in the past, but this one seems different. I pray it's not."

# The Gift of Memories

My immediate family has a tradition on Wednesday nights to watch *Survivor* together. Typically, we record it, so we can fast forward through all the commercials. Sitting down together after church activities on Wednesday, November 3, we start watching around 9:15 PM. About 45 minutes into the "There Will Be Blood" episode of *Survivor 41*, my phone rings. I look down and it's Mom.

"Can you come over? Dad fell out of bed and I can't get him back in. He doesn't have the strength…" she asks fading away with a tone of desperation.

"Yes, I'll be over right away. Just hold tight."

I let my family know we can't finish *Survivor* tonight as I explain the situation. "Do you need me to go with you?" Catie asks.

"No, I can handle this. Put the kids to bed and say a prayer for Grandpa," I say nervously.

I jump in my 2006 F150 and speed over to my parents' house. In May 2020, we purchased their house and they moved into a condo. The house was getting too much for them to take care of and Dad wanted to get everything settled for Mom before he was gone. They purchased a nice, single-story duplex with a backyard right on the golf course, a place he always loved.

Ten minutes later, I pull into the driveway, shut off my truck, and hurry inside. Mom greets me at the door and lets me know what happened. Dad's been on pain meds for his foot, but it was still hurting and he wanted more hydrocodone. In his confusion, he tried to get more meds off his dresser but fell out of bed. Luckily, he didn't hit his head, but he couldn't get off the floor. Mom tried to get him up, but neither was strong enough to accomplish the task. I'm not prepared for what I see.

I walk into their bedroom and face-down, almost naked, and completely helpless lies Dad. I haven't seen him with his clothes off for some time, so I'm startled to see his pasty white skin falling off his bones. There are blood-blotches all over his back as one of the side-effects of his type of cancer is low platelet counts, causing excessive bleeding.

"Tim, I don't know what to do. I just can't get up," he wheezes in a raspy, weak voice.

"Let me help you here. I'll pick you up. Don't worry about it."

I roll him over and firmly plant both of my feet outside his body. As I bend over and grab him under his armpits, a voice goes off inside of my head. *Dad was the one to pick me up when I fell.* Memories come crashing into my head like a water spigot just turned on.

ॐ❧

The last time I saw Dad lying on the floor without many clothes on, I was six years old. Earlier that day, my older brother, Steve, and I were playing Army men. We transformed the living room into a war zone, filled with all kinds of booby-traps. String runs across the ground, pillows in the middle of the floor, an exercise trampoline, and a big, ol' bean bag completed the setup. For hours, we had been shooting each other across the room, make-believe fighting, diving, and hiding from the enemy.

On that same day, Dad was leading a high school youth group on a ski trip to the "mountain" in Montezuma, Iowa. It is a glorified hill, but for Iowans, it is about all we have to ski on. Dad was known for getting himself into situations and reacting in interesting ways. On this occasion, he was riding up a ski lift and when he got to the top, he panicked. Instead of getting off, he stayed on the lift and the chair started to head back down. The weather was on the hotter side, leaving puddles of water with the snow melt. Not knowing what to do, Dad jumped off the ski lift from about 8-10 feet up and landed squarely in a very large puddle. Like a true leader, he skied the rest of the day with sopping wet clothes and his pride more than bruised.

Upon arriving home, nothing sounded better than getting those soaking wet clothes off, so Dad hurried into the downstairs bathroom equipped with a clothes chute to the laundry in the basement. The problem was his bedroom was upstairs and he forgot to bring any clothes with him. In an unfortunate decision, he tried to make a mad-dash, naked run from the downstairs bathroom, up the stairs, and into the bedroom, hoping no one would see him along the way. It was dark in the living room since all of us were watching TV in the family room. Sprinting into the living room, he ran right into the trip line of the booby-trap. Falling head over heads and right into a strategically placed bean bag, he let out a very loud four-letter word, alerting the rest of the family of his presence. We immediately ran into the living room to see what happened and there he lay, in all his glory for us to see. We were uncontrollably laughing, enough for this image to be burned into my six-year-old head.

I so wish the almost naked Dad I see on the ground in front of me now is the result of a booby-trap trip, but it most certainly isn't. I hoist him up on the edge of the bed and gently stroke his thinning gray hair.

"What an awful feeling. I couldn't stop myself from falling. I just have no strength," he whispers to me.

☙❧

Dad had a pretty ridiculous history of falling. I've seen him fall out of trees, off roofs, and down our driveway. But the one that takes the cake is a notorious fall Dad took preparing for a family vacation. Like a lot of families in the 80s, we had the glorious green station wagon, with hot leather seats that burned your exposed skin when you tried to slide on them in the summer. We were heading out of town and needed more storage space for our luggage, so to be even cooler, we had the "hamburger" luggage compartment one could strap on top of the station wagon. Why "hamburger" you ask? Because it looked like a hamburger sitting on top of the car, with its brown and tan colors on full display.

In our house, we had an extra storage area above our breezeway, only accessed from the garage. Dad decided he was going to get the hamburger down from the storage space, so he put a ladder between the parked station wagon and the wall. Up he climbed on the old, rickety wooden ladder. Grabbing the hamburger and pulling it backward, he lost his balance and knew he was going down. In a split second, he had a choice to make. Try to fall in front of the station wagon or try to jump over it. Knowing his momentum was carrying him towards the car, he chose the second option. Unfortunately, Dad's athletic ability wasn't what it used to be and instead of clearing the car, he fell directly onto the windshield, right shoulder first. We heard a CRASH and immediately ran into the garage to find Dad lying in the windshield. Truly, he couldn't have hit it more squarely, making a perfect imprint of his entire right shoulder in the non-pliable glass. We rolled him out and got him to the hospital, and by the grace of God, his injuries were pretty minor in the grand scheme of things.

෨ඉ

I sit with him in the bed and hold his head in my arms. He starts to cry and says, "I don't know what to do. I'm scared. This is just so hard." A wave of emotion comes over me. Parents are supposed to have all the answers. The memory slide show stops on a different memory, one where Dad did know what to do.

෨ඉ

Growing up, we lived next to a rundown greenhouse, always attracting critters to our yard. On one particular occasion, our flower bed became a home to a family of groundhogs.

"I'm going to shoot those groundhogs," Dad claimed.

"You can't shoot a gun in town, Denny," Mom counseled. "Why don't we just trap them?'

"It is the Fourth of July weekend, and people will just think it is fireworks. I'm going to shoot them," he said with confidence.

Dad was not much of a hunter. I personally never went hunting with him nor did I ever remember him going hunting. But, on one of their first dates, Dad took Mom, a city girl by trade, on a rabbit hunt. When he killed a rabbit, he stepped on its head and yanked the body off, and then handed it to Mom to carry. Dad sure knew the way to a girl's heart! I say all of this to demonstrate that Dad's hunting techniques were questionable from the start.

His scheme for this hunt was to lay in a chaise lounge chair in our storage garage facing the notorious flower bed. He would patiently wait until the biggest groundhog made an appearance and then take his shot with his bolt-action shotgun. Setting up his bunker, he lay down in the chaise lounge and laid his shotgun across his chest. We let him be and played inside so we wouldn't scare the groundhogs away.

A few hours passed before Mom saw a groundhog out the window. She called us over to see, anxiously anticipating the coming execution. Any minute now. But, time passed without a shot.

"Steve, go through the garage and check to make sure your dad is alright," Mom said to my brother. "He should have shot by now."

Our garage connected to the storage shed, but no door existed between the two. They did share the same roof, so one could hear over the shared roof. Steve quietly walked into the garage and started to gently knock on the wood wall between the two spaces.

"Dad?" Steve whispered. "Dad, are you there?"

No reply. Then, the snoring could be heard on the other side of the wall.

"Dad. Dad. DAD. Wake up! The groundhog is right outside your door. Dad…" Steve said with a bit more urgency.

All of a sudden, the snoring stopped followed by confused noises as Dad got his bearings. Another four-letter word got muttered and then BOOM, a shotgun blast filled the air. We kids looked out the window to see the groundhog scamper back in the hole unscathed, but Mom's hostas sure took a direct hit! So much for the hunting escapade. Mom then convinced Dad that trapping was a better option. We caught the groundhogs a few days later and released them in some woods miles from our home.

❧

Back on the edge of the bed, I continue to gently stroke Dad's hair and calmly cry.

"Dad, we are going to get through this. I don't know what will happen next but know we are here for you. You aren't alone. We are going to get through this," I say.

"I love you all so much. I'm sorry you have to see me like this," Dad cries back to me.

"Dad, don't you be sorry for anything. We are going to get through this together. I think right now, we just need to pray. Can I pray for us?"

"That would be great," Dad whispers.

Mom comes over and joins us, laying her hands on Dad's shoulders. I pray a powerful prayer, asking for God's will to happen and no matter what, for Him to give us the strength to walk through this together. For Dad to not be scared and for him to know he isn't alone. I ask for obedience, not outcomes, as this is bigger than us. I end by stating that we trust the plan and we will go where God asks. It comes straight from my heart, and I know it reaches the heavens.

I tuck Dad back in, kiss him on the head, and let him know I love him and will check on him tomorrow. I close the door and have a private conversation with Mom.

"We did go to the hospital on Monday and then again today since Dad's foot continues to get worse. At first, they thought it might be an infection, so they upped his antibiotics on Monday. Today, they think it might be bleeding in his foot or something with his platelets. They aren't sure at this point, but they gave us some additional medications, including the pain pills he is taking, and sent us home," Mom calmly says to me.

"Ok, well, that is good. We can't let this bleeding keep happening as he could bleed out. That foot looks incredibly painful. Let's see what the next couple of days bring and go from there."

I ask her how she's doing, and she says that she is ok, but it is hard to watch Dad in pain. I hug her, let her know I love her, and say to call me if anything happens. I walk back to my truck, get into the cab, and just lose it. The entire time I was in the house, I was calm, collected, and doing my best to be strong for both of them. But, in the solitude of my truck cab, I can't hold back the tears. I'm so sad.

It is about 10:30 PM, and I need to talk to someone before coming home to Catie and my two kids. I pick up my cell phone and call my older brother.

"Steve, this is Tim. I'm leaving Mom and Dad's house right now and… and… Dad is dying. He fell out of bed tonight and couldn't get himself off the ground. He was just lying there." I can barely make out the words and the sobs are loud and real.

"Oh. It has gotten that bad. I talked to Mom, and she said something about Dad's foot. You think it is bad?" Steve says.

"Yes, it isn't just the foot. There is nothing left in the tank. I saw Dad pretty much naked tonight. He is skin and bones. His hair is falling out. He has always had such a thick head of hair, and it is barely there anymore. I have no idea how he is going to walk again."

"Well, thanks for going over tonight. After school tomorrow, I can drive home and stay with them through the weekend. We then can see how it goes and help make decisions," he says.

"That sounds good. The thing that got me tonight… I just kept thinking of myself as a little kid when I fell and Dad picked me up. He is supposed to be the one picking me up. Not me coming to pick him up. This is Dad! It's just…" I can't finish as the tears flow.

"I know. It is hard. Let me come down and help. I can take off from school as much as I need to be there. We can then figure out the next steps."

"Ok, sounds good. I love you. Thanks, Steve."

"Love you, too, Tim. Thanks for being there tonight."

# The Gift of Compassion

It is Friday, a week after the first line appeared on Dad's foot. Now, his foot is full-on red, black, blue, and purple, starting from the knuckle of all his toes and continuing to just below his ankle. It is extremely painful, and he has zero desire to get out of his chair. Mom purchased a urination bottle, so the only real reason he has to get up is to go number two.

Over the past 10 years, Dad has grown very accustomed to hospital visits, which is why I was so startled about him not wanting to go to the hospital this time for medical treatment. With all his experience, I think Dad knows this one is different. Sitting in the living room of their duplex, Steve, Mom, and I engage in a delicate dance, knowing Dad needs to get to the hospital, but also wanting to be respectful of his wishes.

"Dad, I think we should go back to the hospital. Your foot is getting worse," I tell him.

"I was there on Monday, and they couldn't find anything. They marked my foot to see if the swelling increased. I don't think it is much worse at this point. I've been in and out of the hospital so much. I just want to sit in the chair," Dad sternly says back.

"Yeah, but you can't even get up from the chair. And your platelets are low, so what if the blood continues to leak into your foot?" I plead.

"I'm not going to the hospital right now. Just give me time to think," Dad declares, and I let it go for the moment.

The journey to this point seems both fast and slow. When dad was around 68 years old, he developed a disease called Polycythemia-Vera (PV), a rare blood disorder that increases production of all blood cells, particularly red blood cells. The increase in blood cells makes the blood thicker. It is caused by a genetic mutation, it is not inherited, and no one knows why it happens.

PV was manageable as it caused him no discomfort or pain. Every week or two, he'd go to the infusion center for a phlebotomy, a fancy name for taking blood from the system. This would reduce his iron counts and thin his blood. To be honest, I don't think Dad or any of us truly understood how serious the disease was at the time or that PV had a chance to turn into something much more serious, Myelofibrosis, a form of chronic leukemia. Cancer. This isn't a word anyone wants to hear, and when Dad received that news, he took it the same as everyone else: completely shocked.

When PV progresses to Myelofibrosis, everything switches in the red blood cells. Instead of producing too much, the bone marrow is scarred and unable to produce the needed red blood cells to carry oxygen throughout the blood. It is a terminal diagnosis; they can treat the symptoms but not the actual disease through regular blood transfusions and medicine. When Dad was given his diagnosis, the doctors said he had three to five years left with the help of a medication called Jakifi and one to two years without it.

I can see the physical toll that living with cancer has had on him. Over the past five years, Dad has received over 130 blood transfusions, with the period of time between transfusions becoming closer and closer. The disease has taxed his immune system with so many infections. At one point, he landed in the hospital for months, with a nasty case of salmonella that a normal immune system would have easily fought off. He got shingles. And the worst one, he developed chronic gout, moving from joint to joint starting in his feet to his hands. The only way to treat any of these infections is through medicine, but then the medicine is killing his organs.

After a few years, it's like chasing your tail. Take this medicine for this infection, and then take this medicine to fight the side effects of the first medicine. More recently, he's been battling another major side effect of the cancer: an enlarged spleen, which has pushed into his stomach and makes it difficult to eat food. This, in combination with the lack of exercise because of extreme exhaustion, means Dad has lost considerable weight.

His body is wearing out, and he knows it.

⮞⮜

Reflecting back, I remember this isn't the first conversation I've had with Dad about getting someone to the hospital. Although the setting for that conversation was much different.

It was March 3, 2013, and Mom, Dad, and I were in Pignon, Haiti, serving together. The day started hopeful as we were heading to a rural village of Savanette to look at a new piece of ground we had purchased and would soon be breaking ground on to build a campus. On the drive out, we pulled over to talk with Metelus, the middle-aged husband of a couple we had recently built a new house for after a devastating fire in their previous home.

"Hey friend, how are you doing this morning?" we asked through a translator.

"I'm fine, by the grace of God. But my wife, Annalise, is not doing well," he said back.

"Oh really? What is the matter? Is there anything we can help with?"

"She has been bleeding between her legs for many, many days. Not the normal kind. We can't get it to stop and she is extremely weak," he said strangely without much emotion.

We knew the couple was on a new Health Development Account, providing insurance for the neediest, and if there was a problem, we could get her to the hospital. Many times, the most vulnerable don't understand when they should go to the hospital since without this kind of program, it isn't much of an option for them because they can't pay.

We pulled over and started walking to the house; we noticed Annalise was not inside. Instead, she had pulled herself out of bed and dragged herself behind the house. She was lying face down in the dirt, flies hovering around, and only partially clothed. She was alive but not very responsive and in need of help.

"What do we do?" I asked my parents.

"I think we should pray for her," Dad said and proceeded to lead us in prayer.

After a time of prayer and discussion with Metalus and his neighbors, we decided it would be best to get Annalise to the hospital. She was in no condition to walk, so I picked her up in my arms and carried her to the truck. Her body was nothing but skin and bones, and I later learned this 5'8" lady weighed all of 90 pounds. I placed her in the back seat of the truck cab with my mother holding her, and we drove to the hospital.

It didn't take long for the smell to hit me: dirt, blood, and feces mixed together on old, ragged clothes. I about vomited in the truck as the pungent smell seared my nostrils. I kept praying to be strong enough and not throw up – to be the hands and feet of Jesus in this tough situation.

We arrived at the hospital and again, there was no way Annalise could walk. Scooping her up in my arms, I carried her into the hospital, trying to find help. She was so weak; I had never carried someone so frail at that point in my life.

After a considerable wait, she was finally seen by a nurse and her information taken for examination.

"What is your birthday?" the nurse asked her. A blank stare came back from Annalise.

"I don't know," she whispered.

"How long has this been happening?" the nurse asked the next question.

"I don't remember," she said.

On and on this went, and we began to realize sometimes the vulnerable don't even have the dignity of knowing basic information, like a date of birth, a birth certificate, and health education. We were told the doctor would be some time, so we waited for him in this tiny, dirty room. The heat of the day and the close quarters of the waiting room contributed to the earlier stench. Annalise desperately needed a bath, so I flagged down the nurse.

"Is there anyone who can clean her up? She has been bleeding for some time with no access to water for cleaning."

"No, we don't do that," she said while wrinkling up her nose.

"Well, is there anywhere we can do it?" I pleaded back to her.

"There is a hose out back if you want," she stated flatly and walked away.

Putting Annalise in a wheelchair we found tucked away in a backroom, we took her through the hospital and out a door in the back. We carried her wheelchair across an area filled with rock, garbage, and animals picking at the trash to a water spigot. It was an open courtyard with around 20 people doing various activities. No privacy at all. We took her clothes off, and I saw the horrors of malnutrition and sickness. She had open sores on her back, bones were sticking out of her body covered by thin skin, and her hips were terribly out of line. We filled up the bucket with water, and Mom started to bathe her. We washed her hair and dumped buckets of water on her to rinse her off.

"We can't put on these blood-soaked clothes," I said. "Do we have anything else?"

"We had a team leave some clothes behind last week to give to someone in need. Let's go get them," Mom suggested. "Denny, why don't you run to the house and get them?"

Dad quickly went to the house with our Haitian interpreter to get the clothes and came back with a fresh set of oversized, but clean clothes. We got Annalise dressed and wheeled her back to the small, dingy waiting room.

The doctor finally showed up for the exam, and we got the news: cancer of the uterus. The cancer was too great, and there was nothing they could do. They told us without emotion that we should take her back home because she wouldn't last much longer. We were all speechless.

I wheeled Annalise back to the truck, and we lifted the entire wheelchair into the truck bed. This time, we had her ride in the back while Dad and our interpreter comforted her. We stopped to buy a cooked meal and water to drink. She was thankful, eating a good portion of the meal and keeping some in the box for later. We traveled back to the newly built home, the reason for the stop in the first place.

When we got there, we lifted the wheelchair out of the truck and into her house. We had a group of Haitian friends go ahead of us to prepare the room with clean sheets. A few weeks earlier, one of our mission teams had built bunk beds for this family. Annalise had been sleeping on the bottom bunk. The smell of sickness hung in the room, but we cleaned and made Annalise as comfortable as possible. I looked over and saw Metalus taking the extra rice from the meal and by hand, feeding some of the young neighborhood boys who had gathered to watch.

Before we left, Dad had something more pressing on his heart besides cancer. He overcame the smell in the room and asked her the question of the day, "Do you know Jesus?" he said with tears in his eyes.

"Yes, I accepted Him to my heart, but I have not been going to church," she answered in a very small and weak voice.

"It is not a requirement to go to church for Jesus to be your Savior," Dad let her know. "He is greater than this. It is what is in your heart that matters. That He is your Savior and you've given your life to Him. The news we got today from the doctor means you will be with Jesus soon. He will heal you for your eternal life. Let me pray for you before we leave."

I witnessed Dad praying for our new friend and shedding tears for her last weeks on earth. She had lived a hard life, having a son die in the Dominican Republic at an early age. After he died, Annalise couldn't deal with the grief and become known as a crazy woman. She was ridiculed by many, outcast by society, and unloved by her people.

Until Many Hands stopped to talk to the couple living in a tiny tent made of garbage scraps, she was an untouchable, a leper of this generation. We did our best to love her as Christ loved her. Little did we know that we were building a bed for her final days and a proper house for her to die in. The clothes one generous person left behind were her burial clothes, as she had no others. It gave us all a sense of peace knowing Annalise was loved with dignity and grace during her final months.

❧❦

I sit beside Dad's chair and see him so weak, frail, and not being able to walk. This time, he is the one needing comfort. What a blessing to have had that day together in March 2013, to know how Dad loved the most vulnerable, and to have that truth dwell deep in my heart. To see my mom bathe a woman in her most distressing time, someone she barely knew, and to know Mom will now walk with Dad the same way through his final steps in life is a comfort. We have been prepared for such a time as this.

"Steve and I are going to go to lunch together," I say to Dad. "When we get back from lunch, we can discuss more about the next steps. Rest up!"

"I don't want to go to the hospital. I think your mom and I can manage," he says back.

I look over at Mom, and she stares at me blankly. I think she knows but doesn't want to force a decision on Dad.

"Don't worry about it for now. Tim and I will go to lunch, and we can all talk about it when we get back," Steve says.

# THE GIFT OF WISDOM

Sitting down at Yamato, a Japanese Steakhouse in town, we quickly put our order in for hibachi New York steak and rice. Steve takes a drink of water and looks over at me.

"He is much worse than I thought," he says. "He can't do much of anything right now. And when he takes these pain medications, he doesn't think straight. His personality even changes as he is irritated and angry. He isn't thinking rationally about any of this."

I take a deep breath and slowly let the air out of my lungs. I've sensed this same thing as well but didn't want to admit it.

"I know. I'm seeing it as well. I know he doesn't want to go to the hospital, but he can't take care of himself at home. And the amount of pain he is in… it isn't fair to put that all on Mom," I reply with a sigh of exasperation. Being in this new reality is fully overwhelming.

Steve then recalls all he has seen in the past 24 hours. The moments that worry us the most are the times when Dad seems confused and does not fully comprehend the situation.

"This just isn't him," he concludes.

∂◦◦6

I couldn't agree more with that statement as Dad always had a sharp mind through his many experiences.

Wisdom and knowledge were gifts Dad shared with the world, both in words and deeds. Sometimes the best teacher is the one who doesn't have to say anything but lives life according to their values. That was Dad.

Yet, Dad never took himself too seriously. Take his two nicknames, for example, given by those closest to him – Carp and Silver Fox. How he received and responded to those names is quite the story.

When I was growing up, my aunt Judy and uncle Dennis had a swimming pool we would frequent often. Countless memories were made with my siblings and cousins in this pool. Mom was a lifeguard and fantastic swimmer. Because of this, I don't remember a time I couldn't swim, and all of us kids were great swimmers. Then there was Dad. He did not grow up swimming and frankly, didn't enjoy much time in the water. But, he was a good sport and most of the time he would go with us to the pool and just sit on the edge, getting tanned golden brown.

On one of those days, we decided to play water volleyball, and we convinced Dad to play with us. Standing on the edge of the pool, he decided to jump in. However, instead of a normal jump, he did some kind of half-jump and half-dive into the water resulting in an awkward belly flop. Then he kind of sank to the bottom of the shallow pool. When he popped back out of the water, his glasses fell off and he spat water everywhere.

Steve yelled out, "Nice, you ol' carp!" Dad didn't refute it. When we started to play the volleyball game, Dad flailed around in the water, again looking like a carp. Steve kept calling him "Carp" the whole game, and it stuck. For the next 30 years, he was affectionately called Carp by most of that side of the family, especially during pool time.

The nickname Silver Fox came from a different story. Dad always had thick black hair, but as he aged, it turned silver. He liked to poke fun at himself, so he would always say, "When you get my age, you can only hope you look this good. I'm a Silver Fox." Picking up on this term, people would jokingly call him Silver Fox. I remember walking into his workplace one day and asking the secretaries up front if Dad was free. They responded, "Oh, you mean Silver Fox?" and then busted out laughing. And Dad just leaned into it. He would pull his small, black comb out of his pocket and proceed to slick his hair to perfect the Silver Fox look and then chuckle to himself.

Dad also had a gift to be present with people in need. This would take on all sorts of shapes and sizes. For many years, Dad was a teacher and high school basketball coach. He was called Coach by some till the day he died. He also was a high school guidance counselor, which included opening an alternative high school in a needy Iowa community. This put him in direct contact with people of many different beliefs, backgrounds, and stories, yet he had a way to connect and make them feel special.

Dad and Mom sang at so many weddings and funerals, I can't count them all. I've been stopped time and time again by strangers sharing how beautiful Dad's voice was or the words of encouragement he shared during a funeral. He made himself available to people on both ends of the spectrum – from celebrating a new life to saying goodbye for the last time. He met each person at their unique place in Dad's unique way.

One of my favorite ways Dad was present to people in need was through teaching adult Sunday School for over 30 years. People would come to Dad's Sunday School class from all walks of life and with all kinds of political and religious beliefs. He would take the sermon shared that day and lead a group discussion around it. And believe me, it could get heated in the room as many times topics veered to touchy subjects with varying beliefs. Yet, Dad could navigate the room, ensuring everyone felt heard and appreciated for their opinions and at the same time, mold and shape thoughts in a Christ-honoring way. Many times he did this by being extremely vulnerable and opening up about his own struggles. With courage, he was willing to ask the tough questions of God and be okay with wrestling through the answers together.

Even through cancer, Dad remained in this posture with others on the journey with him. He had a regular email chain, sharing his frustrations and experiences with cancer. Many grew spiritually because of Dad sharing life with them. He was an open book, showing exactly what he was feeling – both good and bad. He wore his emotions on his sleeve and because of this, many people could connect with him at various levels. The number of cups of coffee he had with people, even in the last five years when his physical health was declining, was off the charts. The baristas knew his order when he walked in the door, with mutual teasing during the exchange. That was Dad.

৯৽৹৻

"I'm going to text my doctor friend to see if he can give any input to help us decide what to do next," I say to Steve. I proceed to text Dr. Spencer Carlstone to give me a call to talk through this, as a friend, if he has time over his lunch hour.

My phone then rings, and it is Mom.

"Hey, Mom."

"Hey. I snuck away from Dad a little bit to give you a quick head's up. Dad is charged up right now as he thinks you and Steve are off setting things up and will force him to go to the hospital. Please don't come back and just say you've made a decision," Mom states on the phone.

"That isn't our intention at all," I answer. "We want us all to talk about it when we get back. I've sent a text to Dr. Carlstone to get his opinion on the matter as I think we need more data to help us decide. Dad is not thinking straight right now, and we want to honor that, but we also need to do what is best for his health and your ability to take care of him. He is helpless right now and is getting worse every day. This is heading in the wrong direction, and we need to do something."

"I agree with you, but please have a conversation with him and don't demand anything of him. He thinks that is what you are going to do, and that he will never come back home," she says back to me.

"Give us a little credit, Mom. We aren't going to force him to do anything at this point, but we do need to talk through this together. Our goal is to get his foot healed as the first step. Let's not worry about all the rest at this point and focus on what we need to do with the foot. That will dictate everything else moving forward. And hopefully, I hear from Dr. Carlstone soon," I add.

"Ok. That is good. Let's plan to talk together when you get back. Enjoy your lunch and see you soon," she says.

I hang up the phone and tell Steve about the conversation. We both are a little annoyed as it was never our intention to take control of the situation without input from everyone involved. My phone rings, and it is Dr. Carlstone.

"Hey, Spencer. Thank you for calling me," I state.

"It sounded urgent. What is going on?" he asks.

"I'm asking you this more as a friend, not strictly your opinion as a doctor," I begin. "I know you can't give me direct medical advice as Dad isn't your patient, but you do have experience in how hospitals work and the entire system, as well as medical experience. So can I share this with you and not put you in a compromising position?"

"Go ahead. I understand and will do my best," he calmly says to me.

"As you know, Dad has been battling cancer for over five years. It is a rare blood cancer, slowly stripping him of his physical abilities. And more than likely, with the lack of oxygen in his blood, it probably has affected some mental abilities in recent months. About a week ago, Dad woke up and had a spot on his foot between two toes. It looked like a small bruise. It got progressively worse over the last week and now is extremely painful and looks like someone took a baseball bat to his foot. He is completely immobile, not able to put any weight on the foot, and screams when we touch it.

"He has been to the ER in Pella twice in the last week, with them not knowing exactly what it is. Could be chronic gout. Could be a slow bleed from his low platelet count. Could be a lack of blood circulating. At this stage of the game, it is a bit of chasing his tail to determine what is exactly happening with his body.

"In addition to the pain, his mental understanding is slipping, and I question if he truly understands what is happening to him. He is deathly afraid of going back to the hospital, as he thinks they will admit him and then he will never get back home. He doesn't want this to end in a hospital at all." The emotions begin to rise as I finish sharing. It's difficult to put that last sentence into words.

"Have you talked about hospice?" Spencer asks.

"No, that has not been talked about," I answer quickly. "Our understanding with hospice is they will only do quality of life treatments and not anything to prolong life. Dad still wants to fight, and if he doesn't get blood transfusions, it wouldn't be long. He isn't at that place yet. We need to figure out what is going on with his foot because if that foot doesn't get better, he can't do anything. And there is no way Mom can take care of him for very long under these conditions."

"Well, if hospice is out, then yes, he needs to get to a hospital to check it out. The longer you wait, the less likely you will be able to treat anything. And the stress on his body has the potential to cause other issues. You can go to Pella Regional ER, but more than likely, they will refer you to Des Moines. If you can get him to Des

Moines, it might be better to go straight there. Especially if that is where his oncology doctors are already located," he advises.

"Just to be clear, in your opinion, based upon your vast experience, we should be getting Dad to a hospital?" I ask to verify what I heard.

"Yes. It is either going to happen by your family's choice or forced by the situation," he says. "As you said, it is getting worse, and under his current condition, it isn't going to clear up. How you get him into the hospital is up to you. Going to Pella Regional is more local, and they know your family better. Do you want me to check who is working in the ER today?"

"Yes, that would be very helpful as it might calm Dad a bit and help him go."

"Ok, I will take a look at the schedule and text you. Do you think you can get him into a car or will he need an ambulance?"

"I think my brother and I can manage to get him loaded up. If anything, we can carry him," I say.

"These aren't easy decisions, brother. I feel for you. Do you or someone in your family have power of attorney?" Spencer asks. "It might reach a point where your dad isn't mentally capable of making these decisions."

"Yes, I do believe Mom has power of attorney for health care if needed. I will double-check with her to be sure," I say.

"We will be praying for you all, and if you need anything else, let me know," Spencer says. "Love your dad well through this."

"Thank you so much for this call. It gives us more data and an expert to reference in the conversations to come." I take a breath and continue, "And it really helps me process. Thank you, friend."

I hang up, walk back into Yamato, and update Steve on the conversation with Dr. Carlstone. My food is cold, but my appetite isn't much at this point anyway. We both know Dad needs to go to the hospital, but the conversation ahead is heavy. We wrap up our time at Yamato, not fully knowing what lies ahead of us.

# THE GIFT OF MEANINGFUL CONVERSATION

We pull into Mom and Dad's driveway and discuss our game plan. Growing up, you never think about these types of conversations with your parents. And then when the moment comes, it is almost surreal. Am I really having this conversation right now?

Going into the talk, we both agree our desire is for Dad to get his foot better, to honor and respect him through the process, and to not force anything. But, we also know we need to be firm in trying to help. I throw up a quick prayer, and we walk inside.

"Dad, I talked to Dr. Carlstone over lunch since he is a good friend of mine. I wanted to get his opinion as he knows the health care system and how it works," I start off the talk. I then go on to explain what Dr. Carlstone told me and his recommendations to get to the hospital to be checked out.

"I just don't like any of this," Dad says, with a bit of disgust in his voice. "I know this isn't good, but I also don't want to go to the hospital because I'm afraid I'll never get back here. I just want to sit in my chair and see if it gets better."

"And what if it gets worse?" Steve asks. "Dad, our whole goal is to get your foot better. It is painful, and this is no way to live. The best way to get your foot better is to get to the hospital. We are on your side, Dad."

"I don't know. They don't seem to be very helpful a lot of the time. I've been poked and prodded enough for a lifetime. And I think your mom can take care of me," Dad says back.

"Dad, let's play this out best-case and worst-case scenario if you stay home." I begin to make my case. "Best-case, your foot naturally heals itself, and you can walk again. Worst-case, something worse happens to you at home. You fall or worse yet, you take Mom down with you. You know she isn't strong enough to hold you up completely on her own." I let that sink in for a moment and continue.

"Now let's switch it to the best-case and worst-case scenario of going to the hospital. Best-case, they see you, give you some medicine, and send you back home. Worst-case, they admit you into the hospital with the goal of getting your foot better. We have to find out what we are dealing with as I'm scared to leave you here. We have no idea what is going on. Your platelets could be completely gone and you are bleeding out. Maybe your circulation isn't working right and this gets way, way worse. I think we need to find out what is happening." Again, the emotions start to rise, but I hold them back.

"Just give me a second to process all of this. When you are sitting in my position, it feels totally different!" Dad says before he closes his eyes, puts his head back in the chair, and lets out a big sigh. I glance at my brother, wondering where to go from here. Steve looks like he's about to say something when Dad asks, "So, if I went to the hospital, what does that look like?"

"Well, there are two options," I explain. "We can go to Pella Regional first. The pluses there are we know people in the ER, and they've seen you before. The minuses are they are limited on what they can provide and more than likely would transfer you to Des Moines if it is more serious than they can handle. Then, once you get to Des Moines, they will have to re-admit you and everything. But, it comes as a transfer versus walking in off the street, so I'd think that process would be quicker.

"Or, we can go to Mercy or Methodist Hospital in Des Moines. They would not be referring you to anyone else and would more than likely be treating you right there. The downfall is we don't know anyone there, and it would probably take some time to go through the process," I let Dad know.

"Bev, what do you think?" Dad asks Mom.

"I think the boys are probably right. We need to determine what is happening with your foot and I can only do so much to help you," says Mom.

"I just hate that we have to be dealing with this," Dad says in frustration, more to himself than anyone in particular. After some time, he comes to terms with the next step. "Well, I think we take a trip to the hospital. I don't want to end up there forever. If possible, I want to come back home," Dad pleads with us.

"Dad, we will do everything we can to get you back to this chair. That is our goal as well. Let's just find out how best to treat this foot and then do all we can to get you back home," Steve assures him.

"I'd rather go to Pella Regional. It is a pain to go to Des Moines, and you are just a number up there. I'd be more comfortable going here," says Dad.

"Ok, we can do that. Steve and I will get you into your Explorer. I'll drive you over and we will see what they say in the ER," I say.

"Just give me a few minutes to sit here before we go," Dad says as he lets out a sigh.

"No problem. We will pack your things in case you need to stay overnight," Steve states back to him. "We will let you know when we are ready to go."

We meet Mom in their bedroom as we gather his things.

"Thank you for honoring Dad in the conversation," Mom says with glassy eyes.

"Mom, we want what is best for Dad AND you. I know the burden this is on you and right now, you can't really help him. We need to figure out what is happening," I say.

"I know he is so afraid that he won't be coming back home. He knows he needs to go to the hospital, but he is afraid of what they will tell him," she shares.

"We can't understand what he is feeling right now. But know that we will do our best to get him back home," I say back and hug her.

We compose ourselves, grab Dad's things, and walk back out into the living room. "Well, no reason to sit around here," Dad states matter-of-factly. "Let's get on with it."

# The Gift of Prayer

We pull up to the ER at Pella Regional Hospital, and I put the car into park. "Stay put, Dad. I'll grab a wheelchair. And I'll have to grab you a mask," I say to him.

"Don't think I could go anywhere even if I wanted to," Dad jokes.

Grabbing a yellow disposable hospital mask and blue seated wheelchair, we go to get Dad out of the car.

"Ouch! Be careful. That sucker hurts!" Dad yells at me as I accidentally stub his big toe on the side of the car.

We wheel him into the hospital, and Mom works on getting him checked in. Sitting in the waiting room are some familiar faces including an acquaintance in town who has fallen off a ladder and severely dislocated his shoulder. He is as white as a ghost, trying to stave off going into shock.

"Rick, you look worse than me! What happened?" Dad tries to break the tension in the room with a little joke. Even at his worst, Dad is still trying to comfort other people.

After a little wait, we get ushered to an ER examination room. The nurse comes to take vitals and get an update about Dad's condition. She hurries off as there isn't much she can offer us at this time.

Dr. Stephen Barnes comes into the room, a neighbor of Mom and Dad. "Denny, what is happening? It looks like you've been here a few times this week. What is wrong?"

Dad tries to explain what he is feeling but can't explain much. He then takes off his sock and the wrap on his foot, exposing the terrible bruising and swelling.

"That does not look good. We better run some tests to see if we can figure out what is going on," Dr. Barnes says.

They wheel Dad back to get some tests done as well as blood taken to get the current state of his blood counts. Only two people are allowed in the room with Dad because of COVID restrictions, so Steve volunteers to sit in the waiting lounge. Once Dad leaves, I go out to update Steve on the latest.

While Dad is out of the room for testing, I pull up an email he sent to his immediate family on April 8, 2021.

*Good morning to all of you!*

*Yesterday I went to Iowa City for an appointment with Dr. Peripu. Dr. Peripu was the doctor who diagnosed this disease exactly 4 years ago this month. It was an appointment that I kind of wanted to go to and kind of didn't want to go to.*

*In the last few months, I have been struggling a little more with the symptoms of this disease. My spleen has gotten very large in the last few months and is uncomfortable. I also think that*

*I am full and I don't have much appetite. When I do eat, I get heartburn and become very uncomfortable. I am also losing weight. I also get night sweats just about every night. My bones are also aching a little more all the time - particularly my right leg. I can't put into words how tired I am.*

*Unfortunately, there has been nothing new that has been developed. Probably the next move will be going to go get another bone marrow biopsy so they can look at the changes that have taken place. They want to know whether it has turned into an accelerated phase or if it has turned into leukemia. At that point, the option might be chemo which I would have to take by infusion once a week. She said that might cause a little nausea for a day or two. The problem is it won't cure it. So if that option comes up, I do have the option of not taking it. I will most likely get that biopsy within the month.*

*I did ask the scary question as to how much time I have left and she said 1 to 3 years. I realize nobody knows when that will happen but the Lord. That number also depends on how fast it is accelerating and also whether it is leukemia. I am a little sad today because I was hoping there was something new that had been developed. I want you to know that I will do my best to keep living and not dwell on dying. You all know that I am ready to go meet Jesus. I am at peace with everything and certainly ready to go. Leaving my family is hard for me to think about – I love all of you so much. We will just deal with each step as it comes.*

*Anyway – just wanted to bring you up to speed.*

*Dad*

I then pull up another email dated May 1, 2021.

*Good afternoon to 6 of my most favorite people!*

*This past week has definitely been an up and down week. I will have a good day and then I will have a day when I am so tired I can't do anything. My spleen has doubled in size the last few weeks which says that my Jakifi is no longer working as good as it used to. A large spleen really affects your appetite as it feels like you are always full. My discomfort with diarrhea continues to make things hard as I am afraid to leave the house. I had a doctor's appointment with Dr. Wehbe on Wednesday. He pretty much told me there wasn't much that could be done anymore. He told me that I had far exceeded his expectations for me and that I should enjoy each day. Well, I already knew that but it was kind of hard to hear it from your doctor. Bev and I had a good chat after I got home – shared a lot of tears but it was a sweet time for me to hear your mother tell me how much she would miss me. We also talked about our will and all those end-of-life things that you have to deal with.*

*Now go to Thursday. I got a call from Dr. Peripu and she asked me if Dr. Wehbe and I had a plan. I didn't know what she was talking about. Dr. Wehbe does not read the reports that Dr. Peripu sends him. She told me to back off the Jadenu that I was taking and my diarrhea would subside. So I have cut that in half. She also told me that I have qualified for a new medicine that was out there that helps your bone marrow produce more red blood cells. That is good news because if that works I can stretch out how often I have to get a transfusion. So this Thursday, I will go to Iowa City and get my first injection. I have no idea what that will be like but I should be ok. You can pray that this works for me – if it does what it is supposed to do, it may even mean that I can increase my Jakifi and that would shrink my spleen. Not there yet but it is encouraging.*

*So that is where things stand as of today. I do have hope that maybe this new medicine will make my life a little better, but I know where my ultimate hope lies – I find myself thinking more and more about heaven as I journey down this road – I have been blessed with 4 years and they truly have been a gift. The thing that makes me sad is the thought of leaving all of you and those wonderful grandkids that you have gifted your mother and me with.*

*Anyway – love all of you so much!*

*Dad*

Reading through these emails again, I reflect on how many doctors Dad has seen and the number of tests done on him over these years. I can understand why he is tired of it all. They wheel him back into the examination room, and he is a bit more disoriented than when he left. Looking exhausted, he lays his head back, waiting for more numbers and tests to determine his fate.

Dr. Barnes comes back into the room and is concerned. "On the test we ran, the one that is most concerning is his platelet numbers. He is so low the count isn't even registering on our tests. This means he is at risk of bleeding out on something very simple. When the platelets are this low, blood vessels don't even work right. He needs platelets. Unfortunately, we can't give platelets here at this time of day; he would need to be transferred to Des Moines."

"Let us discuss this as a family before making this decision," I tell Dr. Barnes.

"No problem. We will keep getting test results back and can make some phone calls as to where he could be transferred if you go that route," Dr. Barnes says.

Once Dr. Barnes leaves the room, I ask if Mom has been keeping Shelly, my older sister, up to speed. Being a teacher in Oskaloosa, about 25 minutes away, Mom was waiting till we knew more and after school was done for the day to contact her.

"I'll call her and get her up-to-speed," I say to Mom. "I'll update Steve and send him in."

I go to the waiting room area and update Steve on the blood results and tell him to go into the room for a bit to talk with Dad. I dial the phone to call my sister.

"Hello," Shelly answers.

"Hey, Shelly. This is Tim. We are at the Pella ER with Dad. It isn't good," I start to cry. I just can't hold it back. "I think you need to get here. I'm not saying it is imminent, but he is not in good shape," I choke out the words to her.

"Ok. I need to find someone to look after Josie, but I will get over there as soon as I can. I'm on my way," she says with a sense of urgency.

"That would be good. We will wait till you are here to make some decisions," I say and hang up.

I walk back to the ER to find Dr. Barnes as he is a personal friend of mine.

"Stephen, can I talk to you privately a little bit?" I ask him.

"Sure," he says.

"I'm asking this as a friend. How serious is what we are talking about? I know no one has a crystal ball, but give it to me straight. We are going to make decisions, and I want to know the truth as we make them," I say.

"It is very serious. We don't see a platelet count like what he has. He could be fine for a time, but it also could go at any time. His only chance is if he gets a platelet transfer," he says with care.

"So, we need to get to Des Moines?" I ask.

"Yes, that would be my opinion. His case is so complicated with all his medical history. It would be better to be close to his doctors in Des Moines. And they see much more of these conditions than we do," he says.

"Thanks, Stephen. Thanks for loving Dad well today," I tell him.

"It is my honor. He is a good man."

After about 30 minutes, Shelly comes through the ER doors, and I meet her.

"I just didn't know he was this bad. I would have come this week," she says, holding back tears.

"No one really knew he was this bad. It isn't your fault. I'm just glad you are here," I tell her with a half-hug. "I'll walk you back."

Entering the ER room, we aren't following the COVID policy anymore as all of the immediate family is in the room with Dad. This is one of the few times I can remember being with just our immediate family. No spouses or grandkids. Just the original Brand family – Mom, Dad, Steve, Shelly, and me.

"Well, it doesn't sound so good for me," Dad states to all of us.

"What do you want to do, Dad?" Steve asks. "It sounds like the only treatment for you is in Des Moines. That would mean they admit you into the Des Moines hospital. I know you have said you don't want to be admitted to the hospital."

Dad doesn't answer for some time and sits with his eyes closed.

"Do you still want to fight this, Dad?" I ask.

"Yeah, I do. And if the only way I can do that is to go to Des Moines, then I guess that is what I have to do. You all would be disappointed in me if I didn't fight this," Dad says.

"Dad, no one is disappointed in what you do. It is what you want to do, and we will support you in whatever you decide," I state back to him.

"I just don't want to leave you all," he cries. "I hate this so much. I was hoping I had more time. I know Mary is going to get married. I wanted to see the boys play basketball. My body is just giving out." Mary is Shelly's oldest daughter who is getting married seven months from now.

Through all the ups and downs of this cancer, Mom and Dad have been committed to prayer. They have never stopped praying. Many of the prayers have switched as they pray less for Dad's healing and more for all those they love to join Grandpa someday in heaven. To witness their faithfulness to each other and pray through all the trials of life is a gift Mom and Dad have given us children. They have always lived the faith, not through words alone, but through action. And prayer became their main tool.

We all grab hands and begin to pray. Beautiful, deep, and heartfelt prayers are raised to the Lord, as God creates a thin place between our family and the heavens. I can feel the Spirit of God in the room as we plead with God to be with us.

"Lord, I don't know what the future looks like for me. And that is ok. I pray for each of these beautiful people in this room. I love them all so much, and it makes me sad to leave them all. I do trust in what you are doing. We love you. Amen," Dad closes the prayer.

"I'll let them know our plans," I say to the group.

In typical hospital fashion, it takes some time for the transfer to happen. Mercy Hospital is full, so he will be going to the Methodist Oncology floor in Des Moines. Dad will be transferred in an ambulance and Steve, Mom, and I will follow behind him. We will run to their house so I can drive Mom up in her car, with Steve driving his truck so he and I can come back to Pella that night. A few more family members show up at the ER in Pella to say goodbye to Dad before he is transferred to Des Moines. Loaded up in the ambulance, we let him know we will be right behind him and meet him at the hospital.

Driving the hour car ride with Mom, it is very quiet. She spends most of the drive in a quiet sob, with the realities of the day finally hitting her. I park the car and go over to help her out of the car. She steps out of the car and just falls into my arms.

"Oh, Tim. I just don't know if I am ready for this," she cries.

I hold her for a while and let her cry. "I don't know if anyone is ready for this. We just put one foot in front of the other. You've loved Dad really well."

"Just give me a little time to compose myself," she says. After a few moments, she looks at me. "Ok, let's go," she says with a firm resolution.

Being almost 9:15 PM, the only entrance into the hospital is through the emergency room. Given Des Moines is a major metropolitan city, the setting is vastly different from our regional hospital. On the outside of the building are very large signs stating that due to COVID precautions, only one person is allowed into the ER. Security Guards are guarding the entrance. We approach.

"Excuse me, sir. Our dad was transferred here from a hospital in Pella. We are his sons, and this is his wife. We'd like to help get him checked in if possible as he is easily confused right now and someone needs to be there to help guide the process," I state.

"Well, you can check with the desk, but I don't think you will all be allowed in. Only one person is allowed in. I will let two of you stand inside the door while one goes back and checks," he says to us.

We slightly break the rules and all approach the front desk. We again explain our situation.

"Only one is allowed back. I can ask the Supervisor if we can make an exception for you. But, that might be a while. Who do you want to go back to help?" the front desk attendant tells us.

"Well, it should be Mom. She would help him the most," Steve says.

"Are you good with that, Mom?" I ask.

"Yeah, that is probably best. I'll see what I can find out," Mom says.

She disappears into the back of the ER while Steve and I wait in the waiting room. After about 10 minutes, she comes out.

"Oh boy, he is so mad right now," she says. "He said the driver must have gone and hit every bump in the road on purpose. And they didn't give him any additional pain meds, so those have worn off. And he said he was freezing. He is not good right now, so I am going to try to calm him down. To make matters worse, they aren't admitting him yet and he is in a little room in the ER. They said they won't take anything Pella did and will have to do all the tests over." She is exhausted and emotional.

"That is ridiculous. I'm going to try to find a Supervisor," Steve tells her.

Mom goes back to find Dad and tries to calm him down while Steve goes back to the Admission Desk to ask for the Supervisor. I stand waiting in the lobby, and a security guard tells me I need to wait outside. I explain the situation to them again, but they say those are the rules and I need to step outside. After about 10 minutes of waiting, Steve gives up on talking to anyone and finds me outside. We are texting back and forth with Mom since we can't talk to one another.

"They just told me his platelets were 28 – don't understand this," Mom texts us. "Still no doctor here."

"Well… you better keep asking questions," I text back. "Be vigilant. Unfortunately, that seems to be what one has to do to get answers anymore."

"Agree – unfortunately, no one to talk to that knows anything – waiting for a doctor!" Mom texts back.

After a little wait, another text comes in from Mom.

"Now they are swabbing his nose for COVID – not a happy camper!!!! Especially with the nose bleeds he's been having – she said she'd be gentle… not possible!!!! Every time he gets relaxed, they come and do another test or something – this is why people hate ER and hospitals."

After waiting outside the ER for a little over a half hour, Mom comes out to talk to us. It is almost 10:15 PM.

"It might be a while yet. Why don't you all go home; there isn't anything you can do here," Mom says to us.

"Are you sure? We can stay if you need us," I say.

"No, he is finally calming down a bit, and they aren't going to let you back. Just go home and get some sleep," she says.

We give her a long hug and tell her to update us when she can.

At 10:39 PM, we get another text from Mom.

*"No doctor yet – probably not tonight. Doctor will see him in the morning. Are going to take him to Powell Room 350. Found out there can only be one person to visit per day. She said last year at this time no visitors, so I should be thankful they have relaxed the rules! They are giving him another pain infusion to relax him. Probably will take him to the room around 11:00 – 11:30 PM. Will get an x-ray of the foot and an ultrasound of the leg and foot. And also check him for blood clots. At least they are looking at everything and will have it to the doctor for tomorrow. Love you all so much – thanks for being there for us. Mom"*

# The Gift of Praise

After Dad is finally admitted to the hospital, we have to come up with a schedule of who will visit and when, as only one support person per day is allowed in the room. Our immediate family texts back and forth, landing on a doable schedule for everyone. The bummer is no one else outside is allowed to be with Dad. Not even our Pastoral Care team leader from our local church. This is especially hard to take since that was the last job Dad held before cancer forced him to resign. To have the person whom he mentored not be able to visit seems unusually cruel.

৵৽৻

Over Dad's lifetime, he held 10 different jobs, ranging from teacher, coach, counselor, salesperson, entrepreneur, owner, fundraiser, and minister. Teaching and coaching were his first loves, and he probably would have stayed in those roles if not for the desire to provide more income and allow Mom to say home to raise the family. But it was his last job that probably provided the most eternal impact, as Pastoral Care Leader at a large church in central Iowa. He took on this job when he was in his upper 60s and stayed until he needed to resign because of health reasons, around age 75.

As a pastor of calling, Dad met thousands of people right in the midst of their deepest pain. He walked many people home in their final days on earth and cared for their families after loved ones had departed. He had such an ability to balance truth and grace in difficult circumstances and help people feel special through the process.

In this role, Dad ministered at a lot of funerals. I happened to stumble upon a recorded funeral from April 8, 2014, for Bob Van Hemert, a long-time member at Third Church. This was before any cancer, when Dad was fully healthy, singing and giving words of assurance to the family.

Standing before the grieving family, there was Dad, with thick, side-parted gray hair, dressed in a suit with a crimson red tie. Leaning against the podium, he addressed the family directly.

"Before I read some selected scripture, I'd just like to tell the Van Hemert family what an honor and privilege it has been to walk with your dad, your brother, and your family. This is not work. This is just an honor. And to walk with someone through those very intimate times we shared the last week, those are special. One never forgets those."

Dad then transitioned to share his heart in how he ministered. Empathy was important as he wanted to be side-by-side with people, not ahead or behind. But, he also understood he could never fully understand what it's like to be dying, and he voiced this with his friends.

"Bob had been in and out of the hospital a lot over this past year, and it was difficult. I always tried to pick out scripture for Bob that would share the promises but also the great assurances. And he knew all of these. But, I also wanted to make sure he knew that we didn't use the scripture as a club. That we didn't beat him over the head with it and these were wonderful, sensitive words from our Lord Jesus Christ. And I also always shared with Bob, I'm on this side of the bed. I'm not in the bed. I didn't want them to come off as preachy. But, I know they take a different meaning when you are lying on your back looking up, and I'm standing beside him and I'm going to walk out of the hospital room. So I always tried to leave that with him. This was all out of love, and that is what it was meant to be. Not something that says you should do this, you need to do that, if you just had this, then things would get better. No, I never, ever wanted him to feel this way."

Then Dad leaned into truth, as spoken from God's word in the Bible.

"I read Isaiah 41:10 to Bob and I'd get through the first part, 'Do not fear for I am with you' and I would stop. I'd ask Bob about what fears he was experiencing right now. What's today? What are you going through right now? And then I'd follow up and say, 'For I am with you. Do not be dismayed, for I am your God. I will strengthen you and I will help you.' And then we'd together say, 'I will uphold you with my righteous right hand.' I always tried to end with that image, 'I've got you right here, Bob. You don't have to fear.'"

Dad then went on to read other scriptures like Philippians 4: 4-7, Isaiah 40: 28-31, and Isaiah 43:1-4, emphasizing the last verse of Isaiah 43:4.

"I read Isaiah 43:1-4 to Bob, stopping before the last sentence. Why has all this been done for you, Bob? Listen to these words from God. 'Since you are precious and honored in my sight, and because I... love... you.'"

Dad always made things very personal. He recounted his last visit with Bob.

"One of the last days when I visited Bob, it was when the family was meeting with the hospice nurse. It was a tough day for Bob, and he had been through a lot. And you know you still have that hope that you are going to get better and you are going to get out of this place and something else is going to happen, but when you start talking about hospice, that becomes a final chapter. And I think Bob was having a tough time.

"By the time I got to him, he was worn out. He was just laying in his bed and I didn't know if he was even awake. So I lean down really close to his ear and I repeated these words to him Lamentations 3: 22-24. 'The faithful love of the Lord never ends. His mercies never cease. Great is His faithfulness. His mercies begin afresh each morning. I say to myself, "The Lord is my inheritance."' I stopped, and I said to him, 'Bob, you know where you are going. You know what your inheritance is.'

"And then in that same posture, just whispering in his ear, I said a prayer over Bob and when I stood up, I knew Bob heard every word because there was just a huge smile on his face. The countenance of the Lord was in that room. It wasn't anything I did, but the presence was there.

"Last Thursday [the day Bob died], was a tough day, as we stood in that hospital room and I was just very blessed to be invited in. And I shared these two verses with the family. John 14:

1- 4 'Do not let your hearts be troubled. You believe in God; believe also in me. My Father's house has many rooms; if it were not so, would I have told you that I am going there to prepare a place for you? And if I go and prepare a place for you, I will come back and take you to be with me that you also may be where I am. You know the way to the place where I am going.' John 11: 25-26 Jesus 'I am the resurrection and the life. The one who believes in me will live, even though they die; and whoever lives by believing in me will never die.'

"And then Jesus finishes that verse with this very key question, 'Do you believe this?'"

Wrapping up the words, Dad finished with this story, one he believed with every breath in his body.

"As many of you know, I love sports and basketball in particular, and I watch all those people cheering after their team wins. Golly folks, we have a lot to cheer about. We win. We know who wins; the last chapter has been written. Bob is now victorious."

❦

A few years earlier in Dad's cancer journey, we had a good conversation about where he was emotionally, as I wanted to know how best to support him and Mom.

"How are you doing, Dad, for real? Not the typical answer you give to someone that wants to give you a minute to talk," I said to him over a cup of coffee.

"One of the hard things I deal with as a Christ-follower is that I know the promises. I have the Scriptures. But, I'm also human.

Mixing the spirituality part with the human part has been hard for me. It is almost like I have the Lord on one shoulder and the devil on the other shoulder.

"And sometimes, I don't know who I'm listening to, particularly about how I should be feeling or what I shouldn't be feeling. There are times when I have incredible sadness…when I just don't like this. I hate it, and if I could give it back, I would. And then I start to feel guilty about the way I am feeling. Maybe I am not spiritual enough?" he asked with emotion. "All these come crashing against each other in your spirit. Your mind can make you think about some crazy things."

"What do you do about that?" I asked him.

"Well, in all the scriptures I used to read to people going through what I am going through, almost every one of them starts with the words, 'Do not fear.' So, I know that Jesus knew that fear was a huge part of this. It is almost like He has to keep repeating it when He is giving words of assurance because there is such a deterrent from us accepting and believing those words. Fear can override everything.

"And what your mom and I have found as the best anecdote of fear is praise. We try to fill our day with praise as much as possible. In the mornings, we put on praise music. We talk about the goodness or things we are grateful for. About the good way God is working in our lives at this particular time. Praise puts fear back in its place."

"How has this affected your walk with Christ?" I asked.

"I feel like sometimes I'm talking out of both sides of my mouth when I go into this area because I don't like the diagnosis. I don't believe the Lord gave this to me. I know we live in brokenness and this is part of being broken. So, I find myself longing for Christ more than ever. And what the devil intended for bad, the Lord can use for good.

"I've been closer to Him than I've ever been. In my quiet time, I've been studying Job, and he said, 'I had heard about You before, but now I have seen You.' This is a very true statement for me. I've known about God for a long time, giving my life to Him at age 16. But now, through this disease, I've seen Him and felt Him. I'm almost sad to say that, as it took this disease for me to get there. But, that's where I am at."

# THE GIFT OF PEACE

Days in the hospital bleed together. Dad has some decent days, but most days aren't great. His mind is slipping, with difficulty recalling events. He is easily confused, not remembering conversations from earlier days. This is tough on everyone. After about a week of him being in the hospital, we hold a family Zoom call for us to talk together and keep everyone up-to-date on options. As a family, it is important for all of us to remain on the same page, even if Dad chooses to go to hospice. At the end of the Zoom call, Mom closes us in prayer. We have difficult days coming, but prayer will be our rock.

### ❧❧

There was a season though, this wasn't the case, and if a breakthrough hadn't occurred, things would have looked incredibly different. Early in his diagnosis, Mom and Dad prayed earnestly for physical healing. They attended healing conferences, prayed faithfully together, and prayer chains were established by friends and family. Pleading with God for a miracle, they waited for God to answer their prayers. Unfortunately, the reports kept coming back worse, with no signs of physical healing, and Dad started to get angry. He was angry at God, Mom, and the whole notion of people praying for him. For a short season, his spirit was going in a bad direction and the rest of his journey could have been very difficult and very bleak. But, about a year into cancer, Dad had a breakthrough. Looking much different than we all thought it would be, as Dad describes it, he had an encounter with God.

"What happened?" I asked him.

"Well, you know this has been a wrestling match for me," he admitted. "You know at first when they diagnose it, you think, 'Well, maybe they misdiagnosed it. Maybe it isn't as bad as they think it is and you are going to get through it. You have had a lot of years.' And then you start to slip and you can see the disease for real.

"So, then you start putting your faith and trust in the medicine. It is going to be the cure-all. Then, after about three or four months, you realize those things aren't going to give you what you need. And I started to wrestle God. Hard." He stops to look at me before continuing.

"I went through this study by Max Lucado and studied the great men of the Bible. It talked about all these great people, and the one common denominator is that they all wrestled with God to find out the answers they wanted. And you start asking the question, 'Why?' However, there are no answers on this side of heaven, and it all boils down to trust and belief.

"But, that isn't so easy either. I've been going to bed at night, and I'd be fearful. During the day, I'd have bouts of great despair and I'd just start crying. And I didn't even know why. Just the thought of what was ahead of me and leaving my family… not seeing my grandkids grow up, or seeing them get married, or graduating from high school. Whatever Christianity I had was not bringing me that peace and joy I was looking for.

"I knew there was an inconsistency between a man who has done all the Christian things in his life and what I was feeling. I've gone to church, I've read the Bible, I've made mission trips to Haiti and done all the right things. But, when I knew I was going to go meet Jesus…" he paused to hold back tears.

"Was I really worthy? Was I good, and am I good enough? Because I knew my motivation behind some of the things I did and it wasn't always pure. They were to bring praise to me and not to the Lord. So, I had to wrestle with all of this."

"Are you still wrestling?" I asked.

"No, I had an encounter with the Holy Spirit," he said completely at peace.

"Can you explain that to me?"

"One night, I went to bed in desperation and prayed, 'Lord, you have to show up tonight. I need an encounter with you. I need to feel what I say I believe.' And that particular night, about 4:30 in the morning…" He paused again.

"This is all strange for me to say," he continued. "This just isn't me."

"But did it happen?" I asked.

"Yes, absolutely," he answered.

"Well, then continue," I said to him with a smile on my face.

"Well, me waking up at 4:30 in the morning is normally not good. I will just toss and turn and think and worry the rest of the night. But that night, there was a peaceful presence of the Lord in the room. I felt the Holy Spirit. And for two hours, I just lay there, and I talked to the Lord. I wasn't hearing audible voices back, but the presence was absolutely there. And I knew in my spirit God gave me this statement and it is what I want to cling to for the rest of my time on Earth. 'Denny, you do all you can do, and I'll do the rest.'

"I knew right then, He had me. It was just so peaceful. For the past months, I've had people in my ear giving me a lot of well-intended suggestions and all that did was cause me angst. It didn't make me feel good at all, and I was chasing their peace by going after what they wanted me to do. And that night, I got all of that out and I was able to talk about it with the Lord. And the next morning, your mom and I got up and we were able to talk about it. And from that time on, I can honestly say I have peace. Even on the days when I don't feel so good or don't have energy, I still have peace. And I am so thankful for that because it makes this journey so much more bearable.

"It has also taught me that this is not about me. I haven't had the physical healing, which I am praying for every night, but I've had healing in every other way – in my soul, in my spirit, and in my relationships. And I am so much better off than before I had cancer. Before, I didn't have peace. And now, I can honestly lay my head on my pillow at night and I can feel good about where I am. Don't misunderstand me. I still want to live and enjoy life. I want more life, and I am praying for physical healing. But, if that doesn't come the way I want it to, I have had healing. And for that, I am thankful."

# The Gift of Choosing Life

After 11 days of being in room 350 on the oncology floor at Methodist Hospital, Dad is getting worse. The bouts of confusion are longer, losing track of where he is and how he got there. Days repeat themselves with no answers in sight. The physical therapist has been stopping by, but Dad doesn't have a desire to rehab his body back to shape. He is just too tired. The doctors are still running tests to try to pinpoint what exactly is happening, but it seems like grasping at straws. All the while, Dad is miserable and hates being in the hospital.

On Tuesday, November 16, I'm scheduled to be the one to sit with Dad for the day, and now they also allow Mom to come as the primary caregiver. We thank God we now can have two people in the room. I drive up early to catch Dad around breakfast, typically when he is most alert.

I unfortunately know my way around the hospital with the number of visits I've made over the last 11 days. After parking my car, and going through the check-in process, I proceed up to floor three and walk through the door.

"Hey, Dad!" I say to him.

"Hey, Tim." Even when he is most confused, he never forgets my name. He is poking at his breakfast, not eating. "This is the pits."

We have some small talk, a quick update on the family, and what he knows about his condition. He complains about a few of the doctors who he feels are rude to him, but he also thinks the nurses are pretty good.

"Those doctors tell me I should be able to do certain things like pull myself up or stand, but I just can't. I physically can't do it. I don't know why they want to make me feel so bad," Dad explains to me. I can tell he is feeling discouraged.

"So, your mom tells me that Jim Danks died yesterday," he continues while looking off into nowhere in particular. Jim was a classmate of Dad's at Central College in the 60s, as well as an infusion buddy because they were both going through cancer treatments at the same time. "I must admit, when I heard this news, there was a part of me that was jealous of him."

"What do you mean, Dad?" I ask.

"He doesn't have to fight anymore. He is done. Tim, this is so exhausting. And it is scary. To not be able to remember things, to not be able to control your bowels, to not know what is coming next. I know it sounds bad, but in some ways, I wish that were me," Dad says as he stares straight ahead.

"Dad, you are doing a great job. I'm sure the burden is heavy for you, and I don't know what it feels like to be lying in that bed," I state back to him.

"No, you don't. I feel bad that I even have those thoughts. I should want to fight more. I just don't as I am so tired. And I hate being here. Hate every part of being in the hospital. If I could just get back to my chair in my own house, I'd sure feel better," he replies.

"Well, Mom is supposed to come this afternoon, and let's have a conversation with the three of us. You rest up," I say to him. I can tell he is tired as his eyes are getting heavy. At this point with his health, he is good for a 30 minute conversation and then he starts to fall asleep. I let him sleep and keep him company.

Growing up, one of my strongest memories is of Dad listening to old Gospel Quartets. The Cathedrals and Statler Brothers are his favorites as I know they remind him of his dad, who sang in gospel quartets around the Sully area when he was growing up.

"Hey, I brought some music and a speaker I think you might like to listen to. We are going to have a concert this morning," I say to him. I turn on the Cathedrals. Dad doesn't open his eyes, but he does lift a finger to show his appreciation.

After a few songs, I ask him if he wants me to continue to play the music.

"I like it," he whispers to me. I let the music roll.

At a little past 10:00, Mom comes into the room to relieve me over the lunch hour as today is the dedication of the newest Many Hands Thrift Store, set to open the following day. I'm the keynote speaker for the morning, dedicating this store to the glory of God and all He wants to do through the profits generated from its operations.

As I kiss Dad goodbye and tell him I will be back this afternoon to talk, emotions flood into me.

࿎࿎

The new store is located half a mile away from where I started life, with my first house being at 4407 64th Street in Urbandale, IA. At that time, Dad was a guidance counselor and the head boys' basketball coach at Urbandale High School. I was baptized about two blocks away at Meredith Drive Reformed Church, where Mom and Dad faithfully attended and served when I was little. Now I am opening a 37,000 square-foot thrift store to support local and global missions right where Dad placed me… and I'm losing Dad. I continue to gain my voice as Dad is losing his. It all seems strange to me.

Walking into the store with around 60 people in attendance, no one knows my conversations from this morning. No one knows the decisions we are going to make this afternoon. I need to pull it together for 30 minutes, to be strong for all the people depending upon me because that is what Dad would do in my shoes. The dedication kicks off with a song of worship, and then I begin my talk.

"As Perry [our musician] was singing, I was thinking about firm foundations. The foundations we stand on today come from so many things put into place way before this whole store was even thought about. It is amazing to me to see how God weaves a story together, winds you around, to ultimately bring you back to places you started."

࿎࿎

This talk of foundations and things coming full-circle reflects not just my story in this moment but also my dad's.

Even though he stopped being a basketball coach by title, coaching never left him. Dad was the consummate coach, always coaching us kids, no matter if we wanted it or not. He was pretty adamant about our shooting form and shooting the right way. Being a youngster who loved to play, my only option to shoot at that point was to go on a 10-foot rim, hoist the ball from my hip, and ruin the form Dad was trying to teach me.

In 1991, my uncle Denny, also a former basketball coach, purchased a very expensive hoop from Indiana called U-Can-Jam. It was adjustable with a turn of a handle, so his kids could shoot with the right form at a reasonable height. My dad and my uncle had always been close and they got to talking about this basketball hoop. Dad wanted one for us, but neither he nor my uncle was that impressed with this very expensive hoop from Indiana. They thought they could do better, with their firm foundation as basketball coaches plus some business background.

With ideas in their heads, they called an engineer at Pella Corporation and had him design an improved basketball hoop. Being blessed in a manufacturing community, they took these designs to a local fabricator and had them build a unit. This hoop then went into my backyard, as the first-ever Goalsetter Systems Basketball Hoop.

Being in an affluent town, people started to see and hear about this basketball hoop and inquired with my dad and uncle if they could have one built for their house. They built a few more and started to sell them around Pella, IA. Someone suggested they should take this hoop to the Iowa State Fair, the nation's largest state fair. They did just that and the orders started to flow in. Being that my uncle had recently been bought out of Precision Pulley, he had the financial capital and accounting background to start the organization. Dad had business contacts and sales background to go work at state fairs and trade shows. And Dad was a natural connector, someone people instantly trusted. From all these foundations, Goalsetter Systems the company was born.

Looking back on that story, so many pieces were put into place way before the first hoop was ever launched. God had uniquely woven a story together and given birth to something in the DNA of my family – helping people play the game of basketball the right way. Dad couldn't have written a better job description for his vocation, and he loved Goalsetter Systems and the family atmosphere they created with people across the country. It truly was a family company.

❧

The dedication of the store ends, and I get into my car and begin to cry. I just feel for Dad, and all I can think about is my healed voice statement. *We choose life. Life on Dad's terms and in God's timing. This is not the end. I'll be the one to help Dad finish well.* How things are going right now is not helping Dad finish well.

I drive back to the hospital and make my way up to Room 350. I quietly pull Mom out of the room.

"Dad is miserable. And he isn't getting any better," I say to her.

"I know. We just aren't getting any answers," she says.

"I keep going back to the conversation we had with him before we took him to the hospital. He wanted to go back to his house. I'd like to have a conversation with him about this. Can I talk to him about his options for making that possible?" I ask.

"Yes, I think we should talk it through with him."

I walk into the room, and Dad is sitting awake. We exchange some small talk about the dedication, and he seems to be following the conversation. Praise God!

"Dad, before we brought you to the ER a few weeks ago, we said we'd do everything we can to get you back to your house and in your chair," I tell him.

"Oh, I'd like that more than anything," he says to me.

"Well, to do that, we have two routes to go. They aren't going to let you stay in this room for much longer. They admitted you here because of the trauma to your foot and that seems to have stabilized, but it isn't healing either," I state. "One way to leave here is to continue to get blood transfusions as you need them and go to a physical therapy rehabilitation center. This will not be in Pella as we've checked and there are no rooms available at this time. They will want you to exercise and try to gain your strength back. Then, if you can show some progress, they might release you to live back at home. Do you want us to pursue this option for you?"

"That doesn't sound good at all. I don't want to exercise. I just want to sit. I don't have the strength," Dad says exasperated.

"The other route to get you home is hospice. If we choose this route, we will no longer treat cancer. No more blood transfusions or anything else to prolong life. All effort would switch to giving you comfort over these coming months. With this, we could do home hospice at your house or go to the Comfort House in Pella. With home hospice, you are at home with limited help from a nurse. At the Comfort House, you aren't at your house, but it isn't a hospital either. There would be access to a nurse 24/7," I explain as slowly as possible so Dad understands the gravity of the decision we are talking about.

"With hospice, can they still give me blood transfusions?" he asks.

"No, there wouldn't be any more blood transfusions," I answer.

He sighs and closes his eyes. After some time, he slowly begins to share.

"I hate being here. This is awful, and I'm losing strength every day. I know my time is shorter than I would like, and I don't want to waste it here. I'd like to talk to people while I still can. Every day I sit in here… for what? So I can get poked more? Right now, the thought of sitting peacefully in my chair sounds wonderful," he tells us with conviction.

"Dad, everything you just stated that you'd like is possible if we go the hospice route. We could probably have you out of here tomorrow. But, we don't want to force anything you aren't ready to do," I say.

"I don't like the thought of not getting blood transfusions, but I'm okay with it. I'm okay with what happens. I guess it is time," he says back, somewhat defeated.

"Dad, I don't see this as you giving up on anything. I see this as you choosing life. Life on your terms. Only the Lord knows when He calls you home, and we can't control any of that. You can control how you choose to spend your last days," I reassure him. "I agree with you completely – we aren't gaining anything here. And if you still have people you want to talk with and say goodbye to, then let's do everything we can to make that possible. Selfishly, I want my kids to be able to see Grandpa. And I know there are so many others who want to talk to you one last time," I say as I shed a few tears.

"Me, too. You and Bev can go and make that happen, as I want to go home. I'm good," he says with affirmation.

I step out of the room with Mom and give her a big hug as we both cry in each other's arms. No one wants to have this conversation, but there is a feeling of peace for both of us.

"I'm so glad he went there on his own. It is hard to see him like this. Thanks for helping him process through this," she says.

"I can't see him wasting away in the hospital anymore. And he doesn't want to go to a rehab center. That would be even worse than here. His body has just given out. There is nothing left," I say back to her.

We get a hold of the hospice representative at Methodist and have a nice, long conversation with her. Most of the hurdles for service we've already gone over, so it can all move quickly, even as early as tomorrow. We determine to start with home hospice and see how it goes since we know it is super important for Dad to be able to get back to his chair at home.

Together we talk through the plan: I will come up in the morning to get Dad checked out of the hospital and get him loaded into the vehicle to transport him to Pella. Mom will stay in Pella and get the house prepared for Dad as hospice will be bringing over a medical bed and other miscellaneous equipment to help us care for Dad at home as long as possible.

After our meeting, Mom sends out a group text to the rest of the immediate family – Steve and his wife, Robin, Shelly and her husband, Jon, and my wife, Catie, informing them of Dad's decision. We make sure all the grandkids are talked with before Mom posts the update on Dad's CaringBridge page. Mom says in her text, "This has been a really hard day but in some ways a good day. Dad is so relieved to not have to fight anymore, but is also pretty emotional."

The next morning, I drive back up to Methodist Hospital. Pulling into the parking lot, I quietly whisper to myself, "I'm not going to miss this place." I enter room 350 for the last time, and Dad has some energy this morning.

"Well, are you sure you don't want to stay here any longer?" I ask him jokingly.

"Are you kidding me? I can't get out of here fast enough," he says. "But, I know they are all going to miss me so much." He points at the nurses.

"Who us?" one nurse says with a smile. "Don't worry, your room will be filled by tonight."

"But, I am sure they won't be as good-looking as me," Dad says with a laugh. This is the first time I've seen him joke for a couple of weeks.

The night before, Mom picked out some clothes for Dad to wear home from the hospital. I pull them out of the bag to give them to the nurses to help him get dressed.

"What did she pack for me?!" he says, startled. "Did she dig into the back of the closet for the clothes I never wear?"

"I will say, these are kind of ridiculous clothes," I start laughing a little. Mom packed a yellow plaid shirt and blue plaid pajama pants, both with very different patterns. "I know she was going for comfort more than looks. Plus, she didn't want you picking up any women now that you get to leave the hospital."

The nurses dress him since he can't even button his own shirt. It is tough for him to stand, but they are experienced enough at this, it doesn't seem to be a problem. Soon, the medical transport company shows up to get him into the wheelchair to bring him home.

"Now, make sure you hit every bump you can find on the way to Pella. Dad likes a bumpy ride; just ask him about his ride here," I say to the medical transporter with a grin on my face.

"That driver wanted me to be miserable. He was going out of his way to hit bumps to spite me," Dad shoots back.

After loading him up, he has one last comment to the nurses helping him this morning. "You are looking at the best thing to ever come out of Lynnville-Sully. You better get one more look before I go," he says with a slight laugh. Dad's love language has always been joking and poking fun at himself.

I grab all of his personal items from the hospital room and follow him out to the van. They situate his wheelchair just right. I take a photo of Dad to send to the family. There is a smile on his face we haven't seen for weeks. Dad is coming home.

# THE GIFT OF INFLUENCE

Growing up, every summer we'd go on vacation to one spot – the Lake of the Ozarks. We'd go with all of our extended family – Grandpa, Grandma, Aunts, Uncles, Cousins, and sometimes a girlfriend or boyfriend was thrown into the mix. We didn't just vacation together; we'd live together all under one roof! When I was young, I never knew it was unusual for 15 people to all live together for a couple of weeks, pulling out hide-away sofas and blowing up air mattresses when needed. Now that I have my own family and understand the dynamics of multiple families living together, I appreciate this even more.

The Ozarks were all about traditions. We had our favorite skiing and swimming cove. Randy's Frozen Custard was always on the menu. Gran Rally go-karts and Putt-n-Stuff miniature golf were going to get checked off the list. And the Oak Ridge Boys cassette tape would get played on repeat the entire week.

There are some favorite Oak Ridge Boys songs, such as "Elvira" and "Bobby Sue," but the one that sticks is called "Everyday." Here are some of the lyrics:

*You know a kind word never goes unheard*
*But too often goes unsaid*
*And on the tongue of the old and the young*
*Gets swallowed up with pride instead*
*You know with all the trouble and sorrow in the world*
*It seems like the least we can do*
*Just take a kind word into the street*
*And share it with everybody you meet*
*And everyday I wanna shake somebody's hand*
*Everyday I wanna make somebody know that they can*
*Everyday I wanna try to show my brothers and my sisters*
*That I wanna help them along the way everyday, everyday*

Whenever we are with Dad, we can not go anywhere without him finding someone he knows or simply making new friends. Dad has a heart for all people and loves to talk with them all. Everyone is important and worth listening to. He just makes people feel special.

So it isn't surprising that when word gets out about Dad's time on Earth coming to a close, the messages and visitors start to line up. When I post on Facebook about Dad choosing to leave the hospital and live his last days at his home surrounded by loved ones, I have 479 likes and 190 heartfelt comments. People long to be with Dad.

"I'm going to put together a schedule to manage the visitors that want to come to say their goodbyes to Dad. I think I will do

15 to 30-minute increments and try to space them out as I don't want to wear him out," Mom says to our family after getting Dad settled.

"How many people have called and wanted to see him?" I ask.

"Easily over 50 at this point. And that doesn't count family," she says. Over those final weeks, 76 people come and sit with Dad one more time to say goodbye because he means something special to them.

"Denny, you were the first man outside of my dad and grandpa that said 'I love you.' And you taught me how to say 'I love you' to other men," comments Dr. Eric Recker, a local dentist in the Pella area during his visit.

Dad nods and says, "We've had some good times. I'm so glad we were able to go to Haiti together."

"Me, too. Those were special times," Eric says back. "You know another thing I've loved about you is that you didn't sugarcoat your feelings to me. I'd always try to schedule your dental visits at the end of the morning because I knew we would be talking through my lunch hour. And I'm thankful for the wisdom you shared with me."

"Eric, I don't think I'm long for this world," Dad says with a pause. "And that is ok. It has been a great life and I know where I am going."

Eric finishes the conversation and leans in for one more big hug, a Denny hug, that so many have grown to love so much.

For a good solid week, the Good Lord blesses Dad with energy and clarity to have meaningful conversations. Even when he is worn out, he seems to rally when people stop over.

Roger Schultz, Dad's first cousin and college roommate, stops over. They are close, being the same age and growing up in the Sully area. As high school basketball teammates for the Sully Hawks, they racked up a 20-2 record their senior year, with Dad surpassing 1000 points for his career. They followed each other to Central College and played basketball together for two more years. Then following graduation, both coached high school basketball and later refereed together. Once Dad moved to Pella, they lost track of each other. That is, until Dad got the cancer diagnosis.

"I'm so thankful we rekindled our relationship six years ago," he says to Dad. Dad nods. "Through all your jobs, you always commanded respect and left each with life-long friends."

"Those were good times," Dad says.

As Roger turns to go, Dad says to him, "I love you, and I will see you again."

"I love you also, and yes, you will see me again," Roger chokes out. He later told me that he couldn't help but think, *This isn't fair,* as he said his final goodbye to my dad.

Phil De Boef stops over, the new Leader of Pastoral Care at Third Church, who was mentored by Dad.

"Denny, I'm so grateful you took me under your wing and taught me what it looks like to give people grace and truth altogether," says Phil. "Jane [another Pastoral Care Leader] and I don't know how you do it! You could tell someone they are being stupid, and then they would say, 'Thank you for that. When can we talk again?'"

Phil would later share one of Dad's emails that touched him deeply:

# Standing on the Shoulders

*Looking at my calendar this morning it tells me we are midway through November [2020]. My goodness, how time is flying by. I must be having too much fun getting old or just being locked down with COVID. You know you are going crazy when the highlight of the week is going to the infusion center to visit with the nurses while they are poking at you.*

*I had an email written yesterday, but I reread it and it kind of reflected the mood I was in – grouchy. I'd be lying to you if I told you I didn't get discouraged because sometimes I do. The good news is that I don't stay there very long as it seems when I get down, I read just the right verse in the Bible that gives me perspective. Every morning I will be sitting down at the table at about 9:00 and I'm doing my reading and connecting with the Lord through prayer. Sometimes I don't feel like it, but I find this is just as important as the medicine that I take. Sometimes Bev and I will sit on the edge of the bed reading a devotion and praying, and most of our prayers are for other people. I don't share these things with you to be bragging, I share them because without my faith I don't know how else I would get through this. Yesterday was a hard day. When you hear the truth from the doctors about how things are progressing, you get discouraged. Then, I think about heaven. That someday, I will enter into the presence of Jesus. And I will no longer be tired. And that will be a glorious day.*

*Anyway – blessings and love to all of you. You are all very special to me.*

At home, Dad has many stretches when he just wants someone to sit by him. I do this quite often as I know he doesn't like to be alone.

During one of those visits, I ask him what his favorite Bible verse is. Without skipping a beat he says, "2 Corinthians 5:17, 'Therefore, if anyone is in Christ, the new creation has come. The old has gone, the new is here!'"

"Why is that your favorite?" I ask.

"Because no one is beyond God's grace. As long as you are breathing, there is always a chance for a new beginning," he whispers back to me.

Each day, Dad gets a little worse. For the first five days, he's able to sit in his chair, just as he wanted. But, his body is failing him and it becomes too much work to move out of the bed. The effects of cancer are now showing in full force.

"Typically with blood cancers, the disease progresses slowly," says our wonderful nurse Barb from hospice. "So, expect him to sleep more, have more confusion, and his appetite will decrease. The good news is there typically isn't much pain. He will have some good days and some bad days."

In times like this, I find it hard to know what to do to bring comfort. I silently ask, *How am I supposed to love him well through this?*

When Dad was first diagnosed, he did an interview on our local Christian radio station. I think of one of the statements he made that day.

"I have to share my emotions with people. And what I want is to get some reassurance from them that 'Hey Denny, we love you.' I just visited Pastor Kevin [Dad's pastor] before I came on this radio interview. And just to get a hug from him and for him to say, 'Denny, we've always appreciated you.' It meant the world to me. That is the stuff that keeps me going."

Loving Dad well through this means showing up, touching his hair or face because he loves physical contact. And most important – telling him I love him.

I remind myself of my promise: *I'll be the one to help Dad finish well.* As long as I do that, it is enough.

# THE GIFT OF BLESSING

It is Sunday, December 5, and in our typical routine, Catie and I get our kids up and we head to church. In God's mercy, the message this week is about a Blue Christmas, addressing those who are celebrating the arrival of King Jesus with a heavy heart. Our family can more than relate as we know the end of the road with Dad is just ahead of us. We are extremely thankful we still had him here for Thanksgiving. Christmas seems like a long way away.

After we finish lunch, I get a text from Mom. "Can you come over now? Dad thinks he needs to go to the bathroom, and I can't get him in and out on my own."

"Yep. I'll be right out. Leaving now," I text back to her.

I inform my family I need to go as we are walking out the door of the restaurant. "AJ, come with me and you can spend a little time with Grandpa and Grandma," I say to my 11-year-old son.

AJ has always had a knack for uniquely caring for people in tough situations. I remember on our first trip to Haiti as a family, there was an elderly woman, super-skinny, frail, and living on her own. Being invited into her house, AJ prayed a beautiful prayer over her. Two years later, we were back in Haiti and in the same neighborhood. AJ spotted her, sitting by herself near her entrance to her house, and he went and held her hand. And again, he prayed a beautiful prayer over her. AJ sees people, so I think it will be good for him to go and spend some special time with Grandpa.

After being sick now for over a month, Dad is in pretty rough shape. Without the strength to get out of bed, the days consist of sleeping, talking, and lying down. His confusion has gotten much worse over the past week, many times not comprehending exactly what is happening to him or around him. To say my expectations are low for a good conversation is an understatement.

"Let's get you up, Dad," I walk into the room with excitement.

"I got to go," he says to me. "I hate that I can't do this by myself."

"Dad, you did this for me for at least a couple of years when I entered this world. It is only fitting I return the favor," I say to him jokingly.

I pick him up since he is completely dead weight at this point, with no real strength to do much on his own. We get him to the bathroom and when he is done, we move him back to the bed. But something has changed. He is alert and cognitively with it. I think the movement and energy exerted have awakened him. In our exchanges, I can tell he is having a moment of clarity and this is Dad back with us as if the fog has lifted.

"AJ, Grandpa is done going to the bathroom. How about you come in and talk to him for a little bit?" I shout down the hallway.

AJ trots in, "Hey, Grandpa!"

"AJ, my man. How are you doing?" Grandpa says with a little more energy than normal.

"I'm doing pretty well. We just got done with church. It was good," AJ says.

Those two have some small talk and I just listen. It is good for my soul. After some time, I tell AJ it is time to go and say goodbye to Grandpa. AJ walks over to Grandpa's bed and puts his head on his chest, with Grandpa hugging him.

"I love you, Grandpa," AJ says in a sincere, innocent voice.

"Grandpa loves you too, AJ. So much. Your grandpa isn't doing so good. But I want you to know how much I love you. Even when I'm in heaven, I will still love you. That won't ever stop and you will always have my love in your heart. And someday, I'd love for you to join me in heaven. Do you know how you get there? Believe in Jesus and that He died for you. Do you know your Grandma and I pray for you every day to accept Jesus in your heart? There is nothing more that I'd like than for you to join me someday in heaven," Dad shares, in complete clarity.

I start to cry as I look at my son being held by my dying dad and the special moment they are sharing.

"You've been a great grandpa," AJ says back to him.

I look at Dad and sit beside his bed.

"Dad, you don't know how much that means to me to hear you say that to AJ. It is beautiful and that is something he will carry with him for the rest of his life. Thank you for blessing my son," I say with crying eyes.

"I just wish I could have that time with each of my 10 grandchildren," he says to me.

"Dad, I see you are here right now, and it is so good for my heart to see you like this. If you think you have the strength to bless each of them, I will make the phone calls. With the triplets Nolan, Summer, and Kaleb going to Central, almost all of them live close enough to make this happen. Do you want me to make the phone calls?" I say with seriousness in my voice.

"I think I do, if you can get them here," Dad says back to me.

I get Mom and explain the conversation with Dad, and that I will make the phone calls to my brother, sister, nieces, and nephews to see if it's possible to get them here. I get on the phone like my hair is on fire, determined to make this happen for Dad and all our family members. I know that family means everything to Dad.

❧

Dennis Eugene came into this world on Friday, April 16, 1943, in the middle of World War II, in a small farmhouse near Killduff, Iowa. He was the youngest of three siblings, with a brother, Chuck, and sister, Karen, and another sister, Gwen, who died at birth. His father, Lyle, and mother, Minnie, both came from very large families, with 21 living brothers and sisters between the two of them. This made for large family gatherings, quite frequent in small-town Iowa.

Life on the farm was pretty simple. They had no TV until Dad was in eighth grade and only one room had heat, the kitchen, so everyone mostly congregated there. Lyle worked the field and was a very competent farmer on his 160-acres. He loved to sing and he also sang for lots of funerals, church, and even in a traveling quartet. Minnie held the homestead together, choring in the morning and feeding the family. She was a very stately woman, never with a hair out of place. She never learned to drive, mostly because when she decided to learn after she had kids, Dad and Karen made fun of her so badly she finally quit trying. Dad always felt bad about that as it greatly limited Grandma's mobility.

Dad went to a one-room school building through eighth grade, graduating with five kids in his class. He walked two miles to school unless it rained a lot and then Grandpa drove them in his Jeep. Dad was a natural athlete, excelling at football, basketball, and track. One thing he knew growing up was that he didn't want to stay on the farm. At the same time, his world was pretty small, and moving far away wasn't something he wanted.

Even from a young age, family was extremely important to Dad. Every Sunday, his parents and siblings would go into town to visit relatives, sometimes out of obligation. As Dad got older, family only grew in importance. Most of his best friends were cousins or other relatives, and he followed them to Central College in Pella. Once he and Mom were married, they stayed around Iowa, minus the summer they spent in Kirksville, Missouri, to complete their Master's degrees to further their teaching professions.

Growing up, I was always around family. Every Sunday, we'd walk to my grandpa and grandma's house for coffee time after church, joined by my aunt, uncle, and cousins. Many times, coffee time would spill over to lunchtime and we'd spend most of the day together. Every year, both sides of my family would get together for Thanksgiving, Christmas, and Easter, filling the house with 30+ people. I never find it odd to be around big groups of people, mostly because I grew up in a big-group family.

Dad, in many ways, was the glue that kept everyone together. When I was 10 years old, I didn't know any different, but now as a dad myself, I realize just how difficult that can be. And it wasn't like there weren't trials. Growing up in Iowa, there are many family splits because of family farm disputes. Dad successfully navigated the sale of his family farm to his older brother, even when it was a bit murky at times.

Dad also navigated the sale of the family business he and my uncle Denny started. Tensions can be high when money and family are involved, but Dad navigated these waters with my uncle. Our family is so grateful the two of them worked through this together and came out of the sale still best friends.

Dad always put family relationships ahead of money, even when it was to his detriment. Someone once asked him what he is most proud of all the things he accomplished.

"My family. To see us all get along, with 10 grandchildren, and to know we love each other. This makes me happy."

A simple life, surrounded by family, isn't all bad.

❧

The grandkids start to show up to see Grandpa, one by one. Nine out of the ten can make it. Steven's daughter Kameron has to come later the same night. Shelly's kids David and Hannah come over with her, but Mary is not able to because of a conflict at college. As the grandkids arrive, I meet each of them at the door with a similar message.

"Grandpa is very present right now. There is clarity in his consciousness, and he requested to talk to each of you. I'm not saying he is dying today, but his window is short. If there is anything you have to say to him, I encourage you to do it now. We don't know what will happen, but we know he is the Grandpa you know right now. Grandma is sitting beside him, and I encourage you to sit near him. He is waiting, go on in."

One at a time, they go in and sit beside Grandpa, saying what is on their heart and for Grandpa to say what is on his. Tears flow freely as Grandpa's love for his grandchildren and their love for Grandpa is evident. Each grandchild has their special time, in their own unique way. One pulls out Psalm 23 and reads it for Grandpa.

*The Lord is my shepherd, I lack nothing.*
*He makes me lie down in green pastures,*
*he leads me beside quiet waters,*
*he refreshes my soul.*
*He guides me along the right paths*
*for his name's sake.*
*Even though I walk through the darkest valley,*
*I will fear no evil, for you are with me;*
*your rod and your staff,*
*they comfort me.*
*You prepare a table before me*
*in the presence of my enemies.*
*You anoint my head with oil;*
*my cup overflows.*
*Surely your goodness and love will follow me*
*all the days of my life,*
*and I will dwell in the house of the Lord forever.*

Others have a hard time making out any words, as they sit and cry with Grandpa. And that is ok as the love shared through these tender moments is enough.

"You know where I am going," says Grandpa. "And I want you to join me someday. Believe in Jesus as your Lord and Savior, and I'll see you again."

Back in the living room, we all gather together – eight of the grandkids, my sister, Catie, and me. Through our grief, we are all connected in a special way.

"Today is a good day. A hard day, but a good day," I stand up and share with the group. "I feel God prompting me to speak to you all as this is a new road to walk. For all of you, this is your first time losing someone you love. It is okay to be sad. I know we all know where Grandpa is going. That still means there is a hole in our lives that he is leaving behind. It is okay to voice this sadness. We have no idea how long Dad will continue to be with us, but it isn't long from now. There are times when you are going to be sad or angry, and I want you to know that it is ok.

"When I was a senior in high school, I lost my Grandpa De Cook. He was very special in my life and looking back, I know I never grieved him well. I made some really poor choices my senior year in high school after he died, and I know it was because I never dealt with the reality and sadness of him leaving. I remember him dying, but I don't ever remember us talking about it as a family. I don't remember any conversations with my parents or any other family members. It was like Grandpa died, and we just moved on. I don't want you to go through the same hurt I went through because there were choices I made I still regret to this day.

"Whatever you are feeling – feel it. It is ok. You don't have to feel a certain way because everyone else is. At the same time, know we are here to support you. Your parents are here to support you. If you ever need to talk with me or Catie, we are always here for you. We rejoice that Grandpa is going to be in heaven. Yes, this is true. But, it doesn't make the hurt less for each of you.

"In these coming days, weeks, and months, please know you are loved. Each of you will grieve this differently, and that is okay. But, do deal with it. Don't keep it bottled inside because it will spill out in unexpected and hurtful ways. That is what I did, and I don't want that for you.

"Does anyone want to say anything?"

The moist eyes look away or to the ground as no one wants to be in this reality.

"That is okay. Let's close our time together in prayer."

After I finish the prayer, I walk back into Dad's room to check on him.

"How are we doing?" I ask him.

"Well, I think it's good. Do you think that was an okay thing to do? Maybe that was a bit much for them," he says to me, always looking for reassurance.

"Dad, that was a Godly moment and a gift they can carry with them for the rest of their lives. You did great," I say back to him with a smile.

He rests his head on his pillow and closes his eyes.

"I love you, Dad."

# The Gift of True Love

It is now Wednesday, December 8, three days after the time of blessing with the grandkids. Over the lunch hour, I pop in to check on Dad. He hasn't eaten much during these past days and is looking incredibly gaunt. He motions me over.

"Hey, you need to listen to this beautiful song," he says to me.

"Oh, yeah. What song is it?" I ask.

"It is beautiful. Hey Bev, can you play that beautiful song for Tim? I want him to hear it," Dad motions to Mom.

"Uh, yeah. I can do that," she says a bit timidly. "Let me go get the record player."

She comes in with a rickety record player and a warped vinyl 45. I have no idea what this is.

"Last year for our 56th wedding anniversary, I bought this record player. I'd found our recorded 45 of us singing our wedding vows to each other. I thought we'd listen to it then, but Dad didn't have much interest in it. This morning during our quiet time together, I brought it out and we listened to it together. It was supposed to be an intimate moment between us, but now he wants everyone who comes to visit to hear it! I'm okay with playing it for you but not every friend that comes over," she says with a chuckle.

She plugs in the record player and sets the needle. The warm scratch of the vinyl comes through the speakers and when the first note hits, we are transported back to August 6, 1965.

కావాగ

Mom and Dad met two and a half years earlier when they were both in band. Dad was the junior drop-out athlete, who constantly forgot his music, sitting next to the freshman all-star musician, who took band a lot more seriously. For Dad, it was *almost* "love at first sight." The problem was that he had been in an on-again, off-again relationship with a young woman named Martha, even resulting in being engaged at one time. Dad never quite had the stomach to completely break it off with Martha. This led to a rather comical first date with Mom.

It was the William Penn College versus Central College football game and my parents' first date was actually two dates. Mom was in the pep band, and Dad sat with her for the majority of the game. But, when the band wasn't playing, he got up and left Mom to go sit with Martha since he was technically still dating her at the same time. Back and forth he went throughout the game, hoping that neither would see the other. To say it was stressful was an understatement. After that weekend, Mom told some friends that she was dating this guy named Denny Brand, only to be told they thought he was engaged to Martha. Somehow, miraculously, it worked out. Dad had to own up to what was happening and broke it off with Martha for good.

A little over a year later, Dad found himself driving around the block multiple times in Pella, preparing himself to ask for Bev's hand in marriage from her dad, Ralph. After summoning the courage, he walked into the insurance agency, found Ralph, and got the blessing he needed. On New Year's Eve, he proposed during dinner, topping off the night by watching *My Fair Lady*.

The afternoon of August 6, 1965, was extremely hot in a church with no air conditioning. The morning of the ceremony, Dad went fishing with his brother-in-law Gary, then home to clean up. It was going to be the last wedding at Third Reformed Church in Pella for Pastor Ringnalda, before he moved on to another congregation. Standing up with Dad was family, very appropriate for him, including brother Chuck, first cousin Roger, and Gary. Mom looked beautiful in her full-shouldered wedding gown, white veil, and three-fourths length sleeves. Dad was in a white tuxedo with a black bow tie and black trousers.

When it came time for the wedding vows, instead of reciting them, they both moved to a microphone and started to sing the beautiful song, *With This Ring (I Thee Wed)* by John Sacco. Published in 1947, it sounds like a song from *Snow White*, with the orchestral strings playing over a full band and strong string bass. It is a beautiful representation of music from that era.

> *With This Ring I come to you*
> *To pledge my heart forever true*
> *I give my heart for you to share*
> *Through sunshine and laughter*
> *Through heartache and care*

*With This Ring I make this vow*
*I'll love you always just as now*
*And my joy will be so deep*
*It can't be sung, It can't be said*
*When With This Ring I Thee Wed*
*Through life's green pastures*
*We'll walk together and love will follow everywhere*
*We'll find a hidden treasure of happiness in our hearts*
*So come with me my darling*
*Let us say a prayer.*
*With This Ring I make this vow*
*I'll love you always just as now*
*And my joy will be so deep*
*It can't be sung, It can't be said*
*When With This Ring I Thee Wed*

☙❧

I can picture my parents singing as I listen with tears in my eyes. The voices on the record are young lovebirds with their entire lives ahead of them. After 56 years of marriage and now sitting together on his deathbed, I can tell that these wedding vows hit my parents differently. The depth of these words has held true, standing the test of time. They truly have been one, until death will do them part.

Raising three kids, both having careers, moving multiple times, starting a new business, and reacquainting with one another after the kids left the house, they have weathered it all together. This last season, in particular, Mom has put her life on pause to take care of Dad. She has been his primary caregiver, emotional and spiritual supporter, and companion. She has held true to her wedding vows to give her heart to share through sunshine and laughter, through heartache and care, to love always just as now.

Over the years, I've had many conversations with Dad about marriage, but none have impacted me as much as what he shares in the last few weeks of his life.

"As you know, Tim, your mother is a very strong woman, probably the strongest one I know. And we are very different. I wear my emotions on my sleeve. She is a processor and needs time to think. It has taken some work for us to really be able to speak honestly and open with one another," he says to me.

"Uh, yeah, I know you two are very different people when it comes to your personalities," I say back to him. "How have you worked through having cancer together?"

"She has been part of the process where I found my peace. One night, we were watching a Hallmark movie together. Now before you judge, at my age, Hallmark movies are just about the right speed and as exciting as I want to get. They are predictable," he says with a chuckle.

"In this particular movie, the couple had been married for a long time. He ended up getting Alzheimer's, and they were walking through the end of life. One night, he got lost and was wandering around, and she went and found him. The disease kept progressing, and towards the end, they were sitting on the couch and shared how much they appreciated and loved one another. And then the movie was over," Dad shares with emotion. I can tell this is deeply personal.

"Your mom and I were just sitting alone at that point with tears running down our faces as we were transferring all the emotion of that movie into our own lives. We got up, moved to the couch, and had a good cry with one another. We shared open and honest feelings about this. We also shared how much we appreciated each other. That exchange softened my heart and made me feel good about what the last part of this journey would be."

*True love is sitting on a couch, holding each other, and being able to cry without saying a word,* I think to myself.

"Your mom has been so good to me. I've grown to love her even more through this disease, something I didn't think was possible. She has taken care of me so well." He pauses for a moment.

"I think that is what I am most afraid of. Whenever we'd travel or something were to happen to me, I'd have Bev by my side. I was never good with directions and she would tell me where to go. I know I am going to heaven, but I don't know how I am getting there. What does that look like to go from here to there? I guess that would be my wish, for Bev to hold my hand and show me where to go. If she could only go with me, I'd be less afraid."

As Dad gets weaker, it becomes devastatingly clear that he will not make it to June of 2022, the wedding of granddaughter Mary. Mary is the first grandchild to get married, and Dad has wanted so badly to stay healthy long enough to attend her wedding. So even though we know he won't be physically present, the family wants his wisdom to be included. My brother-in-law Jon, who is officiating his daughter's wedding, sits down with Dad. He asks him for a special marriage blessing for the couple.

With Mom capturing his words, Dad gives some advice that Jon later shares during the ceremony.

"Mary & Noah - Hold onto each other and never let go. Through the ups and downs, good times and bad, hold onto each other and never let go."

# THE GIFT OF JESUS

After work on Thursday night, I stop by the house to see how Dad is doing.

"It has been a pretty good day," Mom says. "He was pretty confused this morning but seemed to get a little better as the day went on. Your uncle Denny stopped by and brought him his coffee of choice – a Macchiato – but then Dad had an accident and I needed to get him cleaned up. I feel bad, as I think he was going to share some things with him and it got interrupted. Then Dale and Mary Andringa came this afternoon, and it is always good to talk to them."

"That sounds good. Did the nurse stop by today?" I ask.

"Yes, she did and it was perfect timing as with those accidents, he needed a bed bath today. After that was all done and he got some ice cream, Dad asked her how long he has to live. She said it is tough to say, but her best guess would be weeks to months. It is a slow process, but things can change in a hurry.

Since his vitals are stable and he is still eating and communicating some, it doesn't appear anything is imminent," Mom says.

"Really?" I ask. "I don't know if I can stand to see what another month of this looks like."

"I know," she answers. "I was talking to one of my nurse friends with a lot of end-of-life experience. More than likely, at some point, Dad will go unconscious and be unresponsive for a time. It will be a slow process," she says hopelessly.

*I don't know if I can take that*, I think to myself. The thought of an unresponsive Dad and having to make those decisions looms over me. I walk into his room.

"Hey, Dad," I say with some spunk.

"Hey, Tim," he says back, and I'm relieved he has never forgotten my name.

I notice a new, small Christmas tree filled with envelopes.

"Becky brought this over for Dad. It has special memories she wrote about her uncle Denny," Mom says to me.

"Do you want to read any of those, Dad?" I ask him.

He just gives me a blank stare and says, "No."

I can tell Dad isn't here tonight. I spend a little time with him and kiss him on the forehead as I say goodbye. I tell him that I'll come back tomorrow.

Friday night, I bring my family to see Dad – Catie, Abbie, and AJ. We have some small talk, but Dad can't follow the conversation.

"Do we want to read any of these memories from Becky?" I again ask Dad.

"Sure," he says.

"Abbie and AJ, why don't you both grab an envelope and you can read one to Grandpa?" Catie says.

Both the kids go over and grab an envelope and start reading. The memories are detailed stories of past trips and family get-togethers. Dad is having a hard time following, and I can tell he is tired. After each of the kids read one, we agree we will read more later, when Dad has a bit more energy.

Then, Dad's nose starts to bleed.

"Uh oh," comes from Dad's mouth.

Mom hurries over and gets some Kleenex and applies it to his nose.

"This probably isn't good. This is the second one today. When his platelet count gets low, he starts to have nose bleeds," she says to us as she tries to get the bleeding to stop.

We stick around a bit longer, mostly to give Mom support. The burden of caring for Dad can be seen on her face, yet I know she will never complain or say anything negative about it. We all say our goodbyes and head out for the night.

The next day, Catie and the kids have a vocal concert in Des Moines and I opt out of going, wanting to stay closer to Dad. Also, my nephews have a home basketball game at Central College, and I want to watch.

Just after lunch, I head over to Mom and Dad's to check on how he is doing. Mom meets me in the living room.

"He has been asleep for most of the morning. He looks really tired," she says.

I pop my head into his room, and Dad is asleep. For a moment, I have flashes of him in a coffin as his skin is so white. I sit in the room and watch him sleep for a bit, trying to get those images out of my head. I stare at his chest to make sure he is breathing. *I don't know exactly what death looks like, but it can't be far off from this,* I think to myself.

"I'm going to run over to the game. I might come back over after the game, though, before he goes to bed. We will see what the day brings," I say to Mom. She says she's going to listen to the game on the radio.

I watch Central play Coe College, battling valiantly in the first half, but ultimately losing the game. I sit with my brother in the stands.

"Have you seen Dad today?" I ask him.

"No," Steve says. "Mom said he was sleeping, so we are going to stop by before we head home tonight."

"He doesn't look good at all. He is so white and skinny. He's lost so much weight. I know the nurse said she expects him to live a few more weeks, possibly a month, but I don't know if that is even possible. How much farther down can he go? I don't know how his body can take it," I say.

Originally, I don't plan on stopping by Mom and Dad's after the game, but a still, small voice tells me to go back. I pull into the driveway.

Walking into Dad's room, he is awake. In fact, he is pretty alert and I'm taken aback compared to how I saw him earlier.

"Oh, good. You are here and can help try to convince your dad to give me his fake teeth so I can brush them," Mom says to me.

"No," says Dad.

I start laughing. This is not exactly the conversation I am expecting tonight.

I give him all the reasons why he should let us get his teeth out of his mouth and brush them and he finally agrees. Mom walks over and moves her hand toward his mouth. But he just recoils, mouth fully clinched.

"What are you doing?" he asks.

"I'm going to take out your teeth," she says.

"No," he says back.

I laugh again as his face is just comical. It is like wrestling with my kids back when they were toddlers.

"Well, you take them out of your mouth then, Dad," I say between laughs.

"I don't know how," he replies.

"Yes, you do! Just put your finger in there and release the hook in the back," I say, trying not to laugh.

He just gives me a look like I am the craziest person alive.

"You are a case, Mr. Brand," Mom says to him.

"Why?" Dad asks.

"Because you are stubborn. And ornery."

I am almost crying with laughter. In the list of conversations I thought I would have in my life, this wasn't one of them.

Mom and I eventually give up since it is clear Dad isn't giving in. He has stood his ground.

Before leaving, I sit on the edge of Dad's bed. In my time in Haiti dealing with the elderly and dying, I've learned many older people just want to have physical contact as it is something withheld when isolated and alone. I'd often find myself putting my arm around them or holding their hands while talking. It seemed to soothe them and create a deeper connection.

I start to stroke Dad's hair, just like I did the time he fell out of bed and we had no idea what was going to happen next. I think of all the times growing up when I sat on Dad's lap and he stroked my hair or scratched my back. More than anything, I want him to know I am here.

"You've been so good to me, Tim. You have taken such good care of me," he whispers to me.

I kiss him and tell him goodbye, with a stream of tears dripping off my nose. "I'll see you tomorrow."

The next morning, Sunday morning, I wake up to my cell phone ringing. Lately, I've been leaving the volume on at night so I don't miss any emergency calls. I glance over at the clock, and it is 5:25 A.M. The caller ID says Bev Brand.

"Hello?" I say anxiously as there is no casual reason to be calling this early in the morning.

"Something has changed with Dad. I think you better get over here," Mom says quickly.

"Ok, I'll be over right away," I say back.

Catie is awake as she hears the phone ring as well.

"Something has changed with Dad, and Mom says to come over right away. I think this is it," I say to her. "Can you come with me?"

"Sure. Let me get dressed."

We quickly throw some clothes on and get into my truck. Neither one of us says a word as we drive over to the house.

Entering the bedroom, there is Mom, sitting beside Dad's bed. He is breathing very deeply with irregular breaths, not conscious or awake. I can see his chest heaving up and down. Mom comes and hugs me.

"I slept in here last night. I don't know why but just felt like I should. At about 2:00 A.M., he was making some noise, and he had kicked all his covers off. I put his covers back on and got him settled down and back asleep. A little after 5:00, I noticed his breathing switch, and he started to become more agitated. Nothing bad, but he wouldn't keep his covers on. His arms just kept going up and it was different. There wasn't any struggle. I called the nurse, and she said I should give him a drop of morphine to calm him down. And then I called you. I did that a few minutes ago, and he doesn't seem agitated anymore."

"You did good, Mom," I say to her. "Is Steve or Shelly coming?"

"They didn't answer," she says.

We gather around Dad, with me sitting on his left side, Mom on his right side, and Catie at his feet. Tears start to come from somewhere deep inside of me. I'm walking my dad home.

At first, he is taking deep, big, erratic breaths. I watch his chest move up and down as I hold his hand.

"It is okay, Dad. We are here. You can go home," I whisper to him.

The room becomes a thin place, one where heaven and earth meet for a brief time. Mom puts on some comforting, soothing music, the songs Dad requested for such a time as this, when he was still able to talk.

No one has to say a word; we all know what is happening. *True love is sitting on a bed, holding each other, and being able to cry without saying a word.*

After about 15 minutes, Dad's breathing changes again, becoming shallow and faint. His chest is not heaving up and down, instead still and peaceful.

Mom lays her head on his chest and just cries. One more time to be comforted by her soul mate of the last 56 years.

"I think we need to pray Dad home," she says to us.

We gather around, holding Dad's hands and each other, as Mom begins to pray.

"Jesus, I have loved this man all my life. I have faithfully walked by his side in this life. I have held his hand through it all. Jesus, I can't go where he is going. So right now, I ask you to come and grab Denny's hand and take him home. Only you can go with him now. I love you so much, Denny. And I will see you again."

Within seconds of Mom ending her prayer, Dad breathes his last breath, covered in prayer, surrounded by family, holding his beautiful bride's hand the entire time. I look at the clock and it is 6:18 A.M. on Sunday, Dad's favorite morning.

"Is he gone?" Mom asks me.

"Yeah, I think I heard his last breath," I say.

I put my head on his chest to verify.

"He is gone."

Mom puts her head back on his chest. There is a peace in the room that surpasses understanding. I feel the presence of God covering us as He is shining down this morning. What a gift we've been given, and I feel beyond grateful to be with Dad during his final time on Earth. I did everything I could to help Dad finish well. And finish well, he did.

For a moment, we sit together, holding each other. No rushing or scurrying around. Being fully present in the here and now. Words slowly return. Mom wants me to call the family to let them know about Dad. Before we take him out of his house, we want to ensure that any family member who needs to say goodbye to him has the opportunity to do so. A beautiful, full sunrise starts an hour after Dad takes his last breath. God is smiling on us.

We get a hold of my siblings after a short while. They are not easy calls, but they both seem to know when they hear my voice on the phone. After all immediate families have been reached, we call the hospice nurse and the funeral home director, letting them know they can come and get Dad.

Mom pulls me aside. "There are two things I want you to do. First, I don't want to see them taking Dad out of here. So, if you could let me know, I don't want to watch that happen. Also, I'd like for him to leave in his Haiti t-shirt that says, 'Pi Bon Ansamn' (Creole language translated as Better Together). I think Dad would like that."

"That sounds good, Mom."

As they wheel Dad out of the house, I hold Mom in my arms, sheltering her from seeing him leave. It is Sunday, December 12, 2021. I post on Facebook the following:

*This morning, at 6:18 A.M., Dad went home. He was surrounded by family holding his hand at his house. At 6:17, Mom said she needed to pray for Dad. We asked for Jesus to take his hand. At the end of the prayer, he simply stopped breathing. What a testimony for his life! Died on a Sunday, with family at his side, covered in prayer. A beautiful sunrise came up this morning. Today is a really, really hard day. There is a sadness and emptiness I can't describe. But, it is a good day. He woke to a new body. No more pain. No more suffering. In the presence of Jesus.*

*He left this house in a Pi Bon Ansamn t-shirt, which is Better Together in Creole. It is how he lived his life – for God and for others.*

*We will work out visitation and funeral details later. We feel loved by so many and are thankful for the way you have loved our family.*

Over 515 people like the post and over 300 people comment. Dad is finally home.

# THE GIFT OF GENEROSITY

So many friends and family come to pay their respects to Dad and the rest of our family. Having planned his own funeral with Mom's help, it is filled with music, storytelling, and Jesus, just as he wanted it.

For Dad's eulogy, Steve, Shelly, and I share our stories with Dad. I close, following two beautiful times of sharing from my brother and sister.

*As I've been reflecting on Dad's life, I wrestled with the question, "What is the most impactful thing I take with me from Dad?" There is one word that comes to mind: generous. More than anyone in my life, Dad demonstrated generosity in so many different ways. He was extremely generous with his money as Mom and Dad both understand they were just mere stewards of their finances. Nothing was really theirs, so they freely gave to those in need. Dad was also extremely generous in relationships. He always had time for one more conversation, one more letter, and one more cup of coffee. He understood the generosity of his time, and when you were with Dad, that was the most important thing going on. Dad was also generous in forgiveness as he didn't judge people, but rather just loved them. Frequently, he and Mom would take people into their home, offer grace over any past grievances, and love them to a better path. As I stand here today, I can't think of anyone who was at odds with Dad. Not family. Not individuals. Not organizations. That is pretty remarkable to think about in living 78 years on this earth.*

As our immediate family is at the cemetery, leaving Dad's body for the final time, huddled around his coffin, I'm told an eagle flew right over us. Mom and Dad loved to watch eagles as there was a nest within sight of their backyard window. In some small way, it feels like a blessing from God of assurance to let him go.

෨෨

I receive a text from Jon Nelson, my brother-in-law, on Monday, December 27, 11 days after we said our final goodbyes to Dad in that beautiful farewell.

"Hi Tim, would you have a moment to talk?"

Jon doesn't typically text me something like this, so I step out of Catie's family Christmas party and call Jon back.

"Hey, Jon, what is up?"

"Hey, sorry to bother you. Did you get something in the mail from Riverside Insurance?" he asks.

"I'm actually at Catie's parents' house and will be here until late tomorrow night. I haven't checked the mail, so no, I haven't seen anything yet."

"Well, when you get home, can you see if you have something and then give me a call back? I'm not sure what this is." I agree and wonder what Jon is referring to.

The next night, we pull into the driveway and go to the mailbox. Sure enough, there is an official, full-sized envelope from Riverside. I open it up and start reading. My mind flashes back to a conversation from 2010.

❧❧

For a very short season, I worked as a financial advisor, and Dad and Mom came to my office after I had started.

"We'd like to switch all our retirement planning for you to manage," Dad said. "Now you know I am not always the best with this stuff, so I will try to explain what we've done."

He went on to explain, poorly I might add, and then he paused.

"And then there is this crazy life insurance policy. I don't even know what it is, but it isn't good," he said to me, obviously a little embarrassed and frustrated at the same time.

"When we sold Goalsetter Systems in 2006, our financial advisor said we should put money into this whole life insurance policy to the tune of $200,000. He said if we did this and the markets keep doing what they are doing, the policy would pay for itself. We should be able to draw from it later in life and be able to pass on some wealth when I die. It is a $1.5-million-dollar policy. So, I'm better off dead than alive, I guess," Dad said jokingly.

"Well, at first it seemed to do fine. But, then 2008 hit..." he paused and I remember that that was the year the markets crashed. "And we lost everything. We didn't have the money to keep paying for the policy from the gains as the premiums were high, and the underlying cash value lost a lot because we had to draw from it to pay for premiums. We haven't taken a dime from it, and I don't understand how this all works. It looks like it might just be lost money."

The situation sounded hopeless, and I felt terrible for my parents. Needless to say, this particular financial advisor was fired from his firm, sued by multiple people for reckless and undisclosed risk, and was no longer Mom and Dad's financial advisor.

"Oh, man. This doesn't look good at all," I said. I ran the numbers and under normal market conditions, the premium payments would exceed the cash value in just a few years. "I don't think there is much I can do with this. I can make some phone calls, but I am afraid you lost $200,000 on this policy," I said with disgust.

"That is what I was afraid of," Dad said with a great look of disappointment.

"You got taken to the cleaners on this. I'm sorry, Dad."

"This is the insurance policy that I thought had to be defaulted by now," I say to my wife. "And it says we are to inherit some of the death benefit. Steve and Shelly as well."

"Is it legit?" she asks.

"The insurance policy was real. And if what this says is true, yes, it is legit," I say back to her. "I need to talk to Mom."

I text Mom. "Call me when you get a chance." The message is rather blunt, but I want to know what is going on. The phone rings within an hour.

"Hey, I got your text. What do you need?" Mom asks.

"So, I got this letter in the mail from Riverside about a death benefit for Dad. It is that old insurance policy that I thought had expired. Do you know what that is?" I say to her, rather confused.

"Oh, shoot. They sent it to you directly? I was hoping I was going to be the one to tell you about it," she says with a mix of sadness and excitement. "You are correct, that is the life insurance policy Dad purchased when he sold Goalsetter Systems. And yes, it was out of money and about to be canceled. In 2017, we were tracked down by the underlying insurance company. They said we were in arrears of payment by about two years, and they were going to close the policy unless we made payments immediately. Well, by that time, your dad already had a terminal cancer diagnosis," Mom breaks down and starts to cry.

"But, he wanted to give you all this money. We met with our financial advisor and told him the situation. He advised us to jump on this chance to get the policy paid up in full. We ran the numbers, and even if Dad made it to five years, we would be money ahead." She regains her composure.

"We took some of our retirement and put it towards getting the policy up to date. But, that wasn't enough. So, we took a loan against the house to pay for the premiums. We had this all paid for until January 2022, and then we were going to need to decide whether to borrow more money or not to continue this policy," she breaks down again. "But, we didn't have to make that decision. God made it for us.

"Your dad and I talked about this, even this past month when he came home from the hospital. He wanted to make sure it was all in place. He kept asking me, 'Now, Bev, we have everything in order, right? You all will be taken care of when I'm gone, right?' He made sure everything was lined up to take care of all of us."

"Oh my, Mom, I had no idea," I say, floored. "I truly don't know what to say."

"Your dad and I talked if we should share this with you, and we decided to not say anything as we didn't want any tension in you around him dying. He wanted to keep it a secret."

"That sounds like Dad."

"Oh, and here is another thing. You, Steve, and Shelly are all getting the same amount. He also wanted each of the grandchildren to have some money as well. Their money will come to me, and I will give it to them. We will tithe the whole portion of the policy, so you don't need to tithe your money. We wanted to take care of that for you all. And then we will give away some additional money to many of his favorite charities. Dad said he wanted to make sure he gave away over $1,000,000 upon his death to family members, non-profits he loved, and the church, while still taking care of me."

Now, I am the one crying. "I don't know what to say," I choke out the words.

"I know it doesn't replace your dad, but he hoped it would help you all. He remembers growing up in hard times and how difficult it was when he started Goalsetter. He didn't take a salary for a year. And I think it was Steve talking once about the house and car payments and if those weren't there, how much easier cash flow would be. It is your choice how you use it, but Dad was hoping you'd use it to help your family."

After I get off the phone with Mom, I go to my wife and just cry. Cry for my dad. Cry for the blessing he was. Cry for a surprise gift he gave us, in life and death. Cry because he isn't here anymore. If I learned anything from Dad, it was okay to cry. I'll be generous with my tears, both happy and sad.

A month later, my mom is at our house, with special envelopes for my kids. She has gotten into creating hand drawn cards, resurrecting her artistic skills.

"Your grandpa and I have a special gift for you. I know he isn't here to give it to you, but please know that this is from both of us. Go ahead and open it up," she says.

On the cover of my daughter's card is an elegant, hand drawn heart with the title, "To Abbie with our love…"

She opens the letter and her eyes get wide as the largest check she has seen in her short life is made out to her. The card reads:

*Dear Abbie -*

*Grandpa and I have a gift for you. You are being gifted this money with all our love. There are no restrictions, and you can use it for whatever you want. Grandpa and I discussed this, and it brought him great joy to know you would be receiving this gift. You have always meant so much to Grandpa and me, and we hope this gift can be used to help you as you grow up. You have always been so sweet and kind to us...such fun times on Wednesday early outs from school, adventures, swimming in the pool, going to the Ozarks, and watching you perform in sports and music. It has been a joy watching you grow into such a talented and special young lady. God has blessed you with so many gifts and a good heart. I can't wait to see how He uses you to love and serve people now and in the future.*

*Please know you are so loved and always will be our sweet Abbie!*

*Grandpa and Grandma Brand*

# The Gift of Resolution

It is Tuesday, January 11, 2022, and I'm sitting on a hard, brown plastic chair in the Many Hands for Haiti conference room, just outside of Pignon, Haiti. Our eclectic team of Haitian and American leaders are wrapping up a two-day annual planning session as we dream about what is possible for 2022 and beyond. We have one item left on the agenda – in what community should we choose to open our next Love-in-Action Center: a physical, cornerstone building for our work in long-term community development. For me, this one carries extra weight as it is Dad's memorial, funded by his generosity and those who generously gave to his memorial, bringing in over $100,000 for this project.

A month ago during the dedication of the new Many Hands Thrift Store, I had made the following comments to those gathered. "We ignite generosity in others, fueling the transformation we want to see in the world. These stores are places full of donated stuff, and this stuff in turn gives us the ability to help people. That is why we are here. To help people. Opening this store in November 2021 allows us to open a Love-in-Action Center in January 2022. This is a forgotten community of the world. There aren't any famous people living there. It is just a dot on the map for most people. No one is going to travel there. This is a hard place. This is where a lot of mothers have buried children. This is a place where a lot of homes are in shambles, made with sticks and mud, leaking at night when it rains. This is a place where men don't have any work and do not have the opportunity to work. This is a place where, unfortunately, too many children die before the age of 5. But because of this store and the generosity of so many, I can say with full assurance that we are opening a new Love-in-Action Center in January in that community. We take the broken things of the world and we rebuild them, we restore them, and we renew them. We are setting the foundations today to be able to do this in the global world."

Now, our team in Haiti has the opportunity to open a fourth location, and we all want to get this right, setting our strategic direction for the next decade of community work.

The Haitian leaders go through their community assessment as we have been evaluating a community called Savanne Pignon. I ask them to share all the positives they see in the area. We then share all the obstacles to overcome. Lastly, I ask how willing the community is to work with us since transformation is a two-way street. After about 45-minutes of discussion, I make a statement.

"I greatly appreciate all of your work in this assessment. In listening to you talk and listening to the still, small voice in my soul, I don't think this is the right community," I say. I have not told them anything about this center being built in my Dad's memory as I didn't want to add pressure to the decision.

After more talk, we take a vote and decide this is not the community for this time, but maybe at a later date. It is a unanimous vote. We move to discussion around communities we want to begin doing assessments in.

"Last year, we listed two additional communities. Do we move these communities forward and evaluate now?" I ask the team.

"You know, I feel I need to say this," says Pastor Lumanes, our most senior Haitian leader and a very wise man. "I know you aren't going to like this as we have not mentioned this community at all over the past five years in these discussions. But, the need is so great, and I can't help but say something. What do you think about La Belle-Mere?"

My heart skips a beat and I am breathless. I know La Belle-Mere is the one.

❧❧

In 2004, our local church did something crazy. We fundraised for a new building addition and the campaign was called Sharing the Light. As part of the fundraiser, the goal was not just to bless our church but also bless the world, so the leadership team built in a large amount of money they would give away in addition to adding on to the church building. The campaign funds were raised, and it was time to distribute the resources. One of the ways they did this was through a reverse offering. Instead of people putting money into the offering plate, each person attending church that day was to take a $25 envelope out of the plate to go and bless the world, however they saw fit.

Given there are typically over 3,000 people attending church each Sunday, this was more than a bit radical. And I loved it.

Many Hands for Haiti wasn't even a gleam in my eye yet, but my parents, Catie, and I had all traveled to Pignon, Haiti, in the last couple of years. God put on our hearts to combine our $25, making $100 total, and send out letters to our contacts asking them to match our $25 to build a primary school in Haiti. We all gathered our contacts, wrote our letters, prayed over the project, and sent them out with stamped return envelopes having no idea what would happen. Letters started showing up at my parents' house. Lots of letters. When all was said and done, we had raised over $15,000 with our little seed money of $100 and prayer. This became a massive learning moment for me as I saw God come through in amazing ways when you give Him what you have and with faith, trust in Him. We decided to call this school Salt and Light after Matthew 5: 13-16.

[13] *"You are the salt of the earth. But if the salt loses its saltiness, how can it be made salty again? It is no longer good for anything, except to be thrown out and trampled underfoot.* [14] *"You are the light of the world. A town built on a hill cannot be hidden.* [15] *Neither do people light a lamp and put it under a bowl. Instead, they put it on its stand, and it gives light to everyone in the house.* [16] *In the same way, let your light shine before others, that they may see your good deeds and glorify your Father in heaven.*

At this point of ministry in Haiti, we were all pretty naïve about our working knowledge of the culture. We trusted easily and questioned little. We had a lot to learn.

To build this school, we worked through a partner organization as they had a goal of building nine Christian schools in the area. This would become one of the nine. From the beginning, this project had problems. The original budget wasn't close to the actual cost of the school, so more money was needed. Because this was a rural area, the construction went very slow and it was shoddy. In 2007, I led a team into the Pignon area, and we were determined to go and visit this school. After navigating unhelpful people in the partner organization administration, we went out on our own, later learning the reason they were being unhelpful was because they didn't want us to see the school. When I arrived, I was more than disappointed. We were told it was completed, but it was definitely not finished. The classrooms didn't even have cement floors and were a mess of broken chalkboards and benches. I walked away from that school disheartened. It was our full intention to be salt and light in that area and this was not fulfilling that vision.

In all my time in Haiti, I have never been back to that school as I didn't want that feeling of unfulfilled promises in my gut again. The La Belle-Mere community deserved better, but at the time, I had no idea how to make it better. We didn't have the resources, local leadership, or organizational structure to support this rural community.

I know Mom and Dad went at least one time after my trip, only to see the same dilapidated school. They, too, felt helpless, but there was little we could do. In 2014, all of us washed our hands of this partnership organization, stepping away from any financial support of the school. We were heartbroken. We had unfulfilled visions for this community and questioned why God had steered us in this direction in the first place. La Belle-Mere wasn't talked about for over seven years, until Pastor Lumanes said those words. God was up to something.

❦

I sit in the meeting wondering if this was what God had in mind all along. I remember how Many Hands launched our Love in Action Roadmap in the rural community of Sylvain, just outside of Pignon in 2016. The roadmap was built on and established from learning, observing, and doing ministry in Pignon the previous 18 years. I think of the many heartaches and lessons learned that ultimately prepared us to launch something new and sustainable for community development.

This holistic, relational approach gave us true building blocks to help strengthen families to carve a new, better path. It called for us to take an inch-wide, mile-deep approach with geographic saturation in all aspects of a community's life. After six years of staying the course, we've seen amazing results, truly fulfilling the promises we had all hoped for when we started working in Haiti.

Pastor Lumanes continues to build upon his previous comments. "La Belle-Mere is such a community in need. I know it is hard to get to with the river, but the people need help. And I feel they desire to work with us. Every time I preach over there, I sense God calling us there."

The group starts to talk in rapid fire, and all I can do is hold back tears. I let them all first speak their minds. I know my voice as director holds sway over their thinking, and I want this to be pure. After they get done talking, I speak up.

"Most of you don't know this, but this new center is going to be built in memory of my dad. Dad loved this country and her people. He especially loved the forgotten and down-and-out people, who needed the extra love and attention," I say to the group. Then the tears start to flow. Hard. I can't describe it, but I start to weep from my toes. I'm overwhelmed by what has just happened as I feel God's presence surrounding me. And I feel Dad affirming every word I say.

"In 2004, my family built a school, and we called it Salt and Light. We built it in La Belle-Mere as we were directed there through a partner organization. It was built with hopes and dreams for those students and their families. Those hopes and dreams were never fulfilled.

"I visited the school once in 2007, before Many Hands was formed, and it broke my heart. The school was awful, and those families deserve better than what was built for them. Part of the reason I formed Many Hands was because of what I saw on that visit to La Belle-Mere. It is why I am so adamant about the quality of our school, The Sylvain Christian School of Light, and how we treat our families.

"I never talk about La Belle-Mere because I didn't know what to do to resolve the pain I felt inside about this project. It hurt, yet, I felt helpless about how to help. So, I've walked away from it, leaving it behind. And now God, in His mercy, brings it back to me. To us.

"I know what happened in La Belle-Mere always greatly bothered my dad. He so wanted to make things right in this community but was powerless in how. Now, through Dad's death, we have the opportunity to bring life and fulfill the vision he was part of casting so many years ago. Those people in the countryside – Dad loved to be with them. He would love this."

Smiles and tears fill the room as we witness God breaking through the brokenness of our world and giving us a touch of goodness. From the darkness of death comes the brightness of life, moving our world one step closer to bringing heaven to earth.

# The Gift of Legacy

Almost six months after we buried Dad, Mom sends me a text.

"Monday is Memorial Day, and I would like to put some flowers on Dad's grave. I would really like someone to go with me – this is so hard – was wondering if you or your family could go with me? I will get flowers for my parents' grave, too. This all seems so surreal yet… miss your dad so much! Love you – Mom."

We text back and forth and make plans to go on Sunday after church, the same day of the week Dad died. I haven't visited his grave since we buried him on December 16, and it is time to physically go see his grave.

Sunday morning is dreary – one of those days where it can't decide if it wants to rain or not. We pick up Mom from her house and drive to Oakwood Cemetery. I park the car and decide I don't need an umbrella as it is only spitting at this point.

Walking up, I am surprised there is still dirt, not grass, on the site. It makes sense as it has not been a typical spring weather-wise, but I didn't picture it this way in my mind. Mom has not gotten a headstone yet, so there is a plaque in the ground with Dad's picture. Mom has brought red geraniums, his favorite flower, to lay on his grave.

"He always looked out the window and saw our flower box of red geraniums and said, 'Those are so beautiful.' I think he would be happy we thought of bringing him some today," she says.

"I think he would, too," I agree.

After some good tears and a few moments of sharing, God whispers in my ear to tell Mom about the Love-in-Action Center in La Belle-Mere. I hadn't told her about the staff conversations in January and the subsequent assessment for this community as everything seemed too fresh and raw then. Now, the timing is right.

"Mom, I haven't told you yet about a conversation with our Haitian team in regards to Dad's memorial. In January, we were having our strategic meetings and our closing time was about our next Love-in-Action Center. This would be the one we would build in Dad's honor.

"I think you know we were originally looking at the community of Savanne Pignon. Well, after our assessment, that wasn't the right community for right now. We aren't going to build there. As we were discussing the next community in which to do an assessment, Pastor Lumanes thought God was telling him we should look at La Belle-Mere. He said this without any knowledge of our family's history in La Belle-Mere. Immediately when he said it, I knew that this is the place to honor Dad. He would be so happy to know we went back to this community to make things right. I just started crying when he said it as I knew this was it," I say to her.

"Oh, Tim. That is awesome. Wow!" Mom says to me through tears. "How cool is that? Your dad would be so happy."

"When the time is right, I would like for you, Steve, Shelly, and I to go and dedicate this center for Dad," I tell her.

"I'd like that very much," she replies. We both know something bigger than us is happening. Something Dad started a long time ago.

෧෨ඟ

On Wednesday, August 31, 262 days since Dad left us to live fully with Jesus, I am jumping into a black Honda all-terrain four wheeler, preparing to travel to La Belle-Mere, Haiti. It's my first time back since 2007. The Many Hands team finalized on a beautiful piece of ground to build Dad's Love-in-Action Center and want my blessing, with well drilling lined up to start the next week.

This area is extremely remote as a river cuts off easy passage for its residents. No drivable bridges exist, just an Indiana Jones-type swing bridge for pedestrians and the motorcycle driver with a death wish. We approach the river and let the experienced Haitian motorcycle drivers go first and show us the correct path through the water. The current is stronger than I expected as ample rain has drenched the surrounding areas.

"I'm going to wait till the path is entirely clear, as once I go, I'm not stopping," states Craig, our U.S. Missionary Honda driver.

"You realize people pay big bucks back in the States for a drive like this," I laugh back at him.

We take off and the water quickly starts to rise inside the floor of the vehicle. I can feel the tires begin to slip, with a little drift in the back. But, we power through the ruts and rushing water, coming out on the other side no worse for wear. We immediately climb a steep bank, leaning forward in the vehicle to make sure we don't flip over backwards. We are on a mission.

For the next half hour, we drive through some of the worst roads I've seen in Haiti. Calling them roads is giving them more credit than they deserve. We power through nasty standing water that pours a poverty perfume on our vehicle. It is hard to wrap my mind around people actually living here, and navigate these conditions everyday. And most of the time, without complaint.

As we get close to the ground, I spot Salt and Light Christian School, the very school our family built in 2004. It is still operating and now has a sign in front of it. It looks like it was recently painted, giving a much needed facelift to this structure. The tin roof has seen better days, rusted in most places, but I must say, it looks better than I expected. As we stop to take pictures, a crowd gathers to say hello to us. This brings a smile to my face. Dad would have loved to talk to the gathered people.

About 200 yards from the school is a beautiful, wide-open two acres of green. This is the place. I'm blown away with how close it is to the original school. I jump out of the vehicle and walk on my own, leaving the rest of the group behind. This is a walk for me and Dad.

"Well, Dad, what do you think?" I say aloud quietly as I walk around. "This seems pretty special."

I don't hear an audible voice back, but I do feel peace. I walk right to the center to stop and pray. Gratitude sweeps over me as I recall the entire journey with Dad – from being a little boy playing catch in the yard to traveling to Haiti with him as an adult. I picture him in his white Haiti-embroidered shirt, straw hat, and khaki pants stomping through the field with me. He isn't physically here, yet his fingerprints are everywhere. I recall the small book Dad wrote to our family in the months before he died. In it, he wrote:

> *I think my work in Haiti and being with the people in Haiti is what I am most proud of and thankful for. I learned so much from these people who have so little. I saw joy, hope, hard work, perseverance, and faith in my Haitian friends that impacted who I was and wanted to become. I think they helped me much more than I helped them.*

> *I can honestly say I felt closest to the person God created me to be when I was serving in Haiti.*

I finish my time on the land by gathering three small stones, stacking them on top of one another to create an altar of thanksgiving. One stone represents God, another stone represents Dad, and the last stone represents me. It serves as a physical representation of a sacred place and sacred relationship. The center will be a place of new life and a better path for so many families. This is what love in action looks like, a fulfillment of a promise made almost 20 years earlier.

Dad is no longer physically with me, yet I know he lives inside of me and all the impacted people throughout his life. I hear him in the words I say when I speak in front of a group. I see him in the mirror when I look at my reflection. I feel his love at times that I need it. The foundations he helped to build are strong, a legacy of generosity to one another carried on through the generations that follow. We need to give that extra hug, a quirky smile, the handwritten note, and grace for a second chance. To truly be love in action, this never dies.

# Afterword

On June 9, 2023, my mom, brother, sister, and I traveled to La Belle-Mere, Haiti, to dedicate the Love-in-Action Center to Dad. In all our years as a family, I'm not sure we've ever traveled with just the four of us, especially not on an international trip. With no spouses present, we were transported back in time when it was only our nuclear family. Given our busy schedules, it was a sacrifice for all to make it happen, but I was so happy we could experience this together.

It was a beautiful dedication, with around 200 people attending, filled with music, prayer, and heaping plates of food. Community leaders shared the purpose of the Love-in-Action Center and in particular about the First 1,000 Days Program since strong beginnings lay the foundation for a transformed life. Through Dad's death, others will have life, as this program focuses on the critical window of development from conception to the child's second birthday. But, the relationship with the family doesn't stop after this pivotal time, continuing for the next four years. Building off of this initial program, Many Hands invests in providing economical, mental, and spiritual resources for the parents to be champions of their child. The needed resources are provided for the best start for the child's education through preschool and for the parent to be able to pay for it. This is the program Dad had always wanted in Haiti; one that is relational and life-giving over an extended period of time.

As I got up to speak, God gave me the words to say. I closed the talk with these words for the Haitian families in attendance.

*Even though my dad's life has ended, new life is to come — new life for this community, for the children, and for the moms. See, death is not the end for us. If we believe in Jesus Christ, we pass from this life into the next, and we are alive in the next. But, we leave roots in this life. For example, I can go to this field behind this center and burn it. But if the roots are strong, the plants come back better and stronger. So even though my dad has died, he is alive in Christ. He has planted his roots here for you to grow, for your families to grow, and for your community to grow, so that Christ can reign and be made known. And, so that your salt can remain salty and your light can be a beacon on a hill. We planted that school a long time ago, but that was just the beginning. God, in His mercy, brought us back. And now with Many Hands and this center, this community can have life and life to the full.*

We ended the dedication by hanging a plaque near the front of the building, close to the area where people will be loved and empowered and food will be distributed to those who come to this place.

*In loving memory of*

# Denny Brand

## of Pella, Iowa, USA

### Dedicated June 2023

A dedicated servant who sought God's will, serving the people of Haiti.
His actions through the decades had legacy power, laying the foundation
for the construction of this Love-in-Action center.

We can see farther, stand firmer, and love deeper because he paved the way.
We stand on his shoulders.

---

*Therefore, if anyone is in Christ, the new creation has come.*
*The old has gone, the new is here!*
*2 Corinthians 5:17*

---

Pi bon ansanm!

# Your Next Steps

If you were motivated by reading this story and want to ignite your legacy, here are some additional ideas and resources available to you.

**LEARN**

**Read about Many Hands**. I have dedicated my life to starting and growing the nonprofit, Many Hands. We are a global community of people devoted to putting love into action in a broken world. By going an inch-wide, mile-deep with thousands of families, life-transformation in Christ is possible through relationship-based education, leadership development, agriculture, safe homes, medical assistance, and economic development programs. Visit the website www.mh4h.org to learn about the various programs, stories, and amazing work being done by committed people in challenging places.

**Join 3...2...1** Impact Newsletter. Hear more from me in my bi-monthly newsletter, where I share ideas and experiences to help you be people of impact. In each edition, you'll get 3 Points to Ponder, 2 Quotes to Share, and 1 Story of Impact. Visit the website www.mh4h.org/321-impact and sign up for free.

**Visit Many Hands Impact website**. Many resources exist to challenge us to think about our passions, relationships, and legacy moments. Stay up to date on my recommendations, opportunities, and additional resources to do more at www.manyhandsimpact.com.

**PRAY**

One of the themes throughout this book is the power of prayer. I believe prayer is a social interaction with the very Creator of the Universe, inviting us to partner with Him in our everyday lives. Many of us find prayer to be difficult, so I want to provide a little guidance to help you pray.

- If you have problems starting prayer, I pray the Jesus prayer to start, saying "Jesus Christ, Son of the Living God, have mercy on me, a sinner." If you aren't comfortable with this language, start with a "Hey God..." like you were talking to a friend.

- Move into praying outside of yourself. Speak gratitude in the little things you see, for your family members or friends, or the little things bringing you life at that moment.

- Ask God into the challenging areas of your life, those areas of opportunity to be love in action for yourself or others. If you would like God to show up, invite Him into those situations.

- Ask for forgiveness in the areas you have fallen short in your life. Confess the areas where you are not right with God or right with others.

- Close the prayer similar to how you opened the prayer, recognizing that God is more than a force, unnamed higher power, or idea. I like to close with something like, "In the name of Jesus, Amen."

**ACT**

**Share your story**. I've shared a deeply personal story with you, as when we let God's light shine through us, others get illuminated in their darkness. Our stories carry the power to help others on their journey. When I tell stories, I use a simple 4-part method.

1. REFLECT on what has happened in the past. What is surfacing from your past that you believe needs to be told?

2. Then move to EXPECT, which means understanding your emotions around this story, your expectations in telling it, and your desires for others receiving the story. The clearer you can be in this section, the better you can frame your story.

3. Next, nail down the CONNECT section, which is truly the heart of the story. Understanding what has happened and having a clear picture of your desires for telling this story, you now can connect those two parts into something tangible for others. Target a 5-minute story, as remember, this is a gift to another person so be sensitive to their ability to stay focused. Don't try to say everything, but focus on the one-thing you want them to walk away with.

4. Lastly, be firm to COMMIT. Where will you tell this story? Which medium do you think is best to properly communicate the story to others (written, video, pictures, in-person)? Whatever you commit to, stick to it. People need to hear your authentic voice.

Go to www.manyhandsimpact.com to download a visual storytelling board one-pager to help you write and tell your story.

**Be generous**. If one word could describe my father, it was generosity. Generosity doesn't only have to be financial, but it could be in attitude, time, or forgiveness. And remember, generosity is only generous when someone gets more than he or she deserves. Who is someone in your life right now with whom you can be generous? Commit to one generous act a day for one week and see how it changes your life and the lives of others around you.

**Commit to joining the People for Impact Community**. Join a community of people committed to leaving a legacy through their small, daily actions. This commitment funds life-giving resources for people who desperately need to stand on someone else's shoulders for a season. Starting for as little as $10 a month, you will have access to stories, Impact opportunities, and monthly spiritual coaching calls from myself and others on this Impact Journey. Visit www.manyhandsimpact.com to learn more.

**Give beyond the grave**. My dad did something incredible, funding a Love-in-Action Center through his memorial and planned giving. You can designate your favorite charity in your will so that your treasure will continue to be used in compassionate ways after you've passed from this life. Many Hands offers help with this, if you are so moved to help us in our journey, as do other organizations and charities.

# About the Author

Tim Brand is the Founder and CEO of Many Hands, established in 2008. As CEO, he provides vision and leadership for U.S. and International operations. Many Hands impacts 25,000 people in three countries and reaches over 200,000 people per year in U.S. Business as Mission retail stores.

After graduating from high school in 1998, Tim joined a church group mission trip to help build a new school in Pignon, Haiti. This trip changed his perspective on God's global heart. Two years later in college, he was praying for direction for his life and he heard a voice say to go back to Haiti. The next morning, he received an email from a mission team about an upcoming trip. He agreed, and at the end of that trip, made a covenant with God to be involved in Haiti in some way for the rest of his life.

During his time in the for-profit sector, he established an association of Iowa churches working in Haiti, striving to share best practices and financial accountability. It became clear this association needed to become an official non-profit, turning into Many Hands. Tim served as President of the Board from 2008-2011.

Prior to founding Many Hands and going full-time in 2011, he spent 10 years in the for-profit business sector, with experience in global strategies, global account management, IT sales and management, and financial planning.

Tim is an Iowa native and graduated from Central College with a Computer Information Systems degree and the University of Phoenix with a Masters in Business Management.

Selected by *CITYVIEW Business Journal* as one of 20 business leaders making a difference in 2020, he dedicates his life to helping people release their God-given talent to be love in action. He writes a bi-monthly 3...2...1 Impact newsletter, has led hundreds of people on Impact Trips, and steps in as teaching pastor at multiple churches across the Midwest. Tim lives in Pella, Iowa, with his wife, Catie, and their two children.

Printed in the USA
CPSIA information can be obtained
at www.ICGtesting.com
CBHW050830120524
8391CB00007B/28

9 798989 136513